# Flinn Scientific
# ChemTopic™ Labs

# Chemistry of Gases

### Senior Editor

**Irene Cesa**
Flinn Scientific, Inc.
Batavia, IL

### Curriculum Advisory Board

**Bob Becker**
Kirkwood High School
Kirkwood, MO

**Kathleen J. Dombrink**
McCluer North High School
Florissant, MO

**Robert Lewis**
Downers Grove North High School
Downers Grove, IL

**John G. Little**
St. Mary's High School
Stockton, CA

**Lee Marek**
Naperville North High School
Naperville, IL

**John Mauch**
Braintree High School
Braintree, MA

**Dave Tanis**
Grand Valley State University
Allendale, MI

**FLINN SCIENTIFIC INC.**
"Your Safer Source for Science Supplies"
P.O. Box 219 • Batavia, IL 60510
1-800-452-1261 • www.flinnsci.com

ISBN 1-877991-76-7

Copyright © 2003 Flinn Scientific, Inc.

All rights reserved. No part of this book may be reproduced or transmitted in any form or by any means, electronic or mechanical, including, but not limited to photocopy, recording, or any information storage and retrieval system, without permission in writing from Flinn Scientific, Inc.
No part of this book may be included on any Web site.

Reproduction permission is granted only to the science teacher who has purchased this volume of Flinn ChemTopic™ Labs, Chemistry of Gases, Catalog No. AP6366 from Flinn Scientific, Inc. Science teachers may make copies of the reproducible student pages for use only by their students.

Printed in the United States of America.

# Table of Contents

|  | Page |
|---|---|
| Flinn ChemTopic™ Labs Series Preface | i |
| About the Curriculum Advisory Board | ii |
| Chemistry of Gases Preface | iii |
| Format and Features | iv–v |
| Experiment Summaries and Concepts | vi–vii |

## *Experiments*

| | |
|---|---|
| Common Gases | 1 |
| Preparing and Testing Hydrogen Gas | 11 |
| Oxygen, What a Flame | 21 |
| Carbon Dioxide, What a Gas | 35 |

## *Demonstrations*

| | |
|---|---|
| Collecting Gases by Water Displacement | 49 |
| Underwater Fireworks | 51 |
| Flaming Vapor Ramp | 55 |
| The Collapsing Bottle | 57 |
| Solubility of Carbon Dioxide | 59 |
| Solubility of Ammonia | 63 |

## *Supplementary Information*

| | |
|---|---|
| Safety and Disposal Guidelines | 66 |
| National Science Education Standards | 68 |
| Master Materials Guide | 70 |

# Flinn ChemTopic™ Labs Series Preface

## Lab Manuals Organized Around Key Content Areas in Chemistry

In conversations with chemistry teachers across the country, we have heard a common concern. Teachers are frustrated with their current lab manuals, with experiments that are poorly designed and don't teach core concepts, with procedures that are rigid and inflexible and don't work. Teachers want greater flexibility in their choice of lab activities. As we further listened to experienced master teachers who regularly lead workshops and training seminars, another theme emerged. Master teachers mostly rely on collections of experiments and demonstrations they have put together themselves over the years. Some activities have been passed on like cherished family recipe cards from one teacher to another. Others have been adapted from one format to another to take advantage of new trends in microscale equipment and procedures, technology innovations, and discovery-based learning theory. In all cases the experiments and demonstrations have been fine-tuned based on real classroom experience.

Flinn Scientific has developed a series of lab manuals based on these "cherished recipe cards" of master teachers with proven excellence in both teaching students and training teachers. Created under the direction of an Advisory Board of award-winning chemistry teachers, each lab manual in the Flinn ChemTopic™ Labs series contains 4–6 student-tested experiments that focus on essential concepts and applications in a single content area. Each lab manual also contains 4–6 demonstrations that can be used to illustrate a chemical property, reaction, or relationship and will capture your students' attention. The experiments and demonstrations in the Flinn ChemTopic™ Labs series are enjoyable, highly focused, and will give students a real sense of accomplishment.

***Laboratory experiments*** allow students to experience chemistry by doing chemistry. Experiments have been selected to provide students with a crystal-clear understanding of chemistry concepts and encourage students to think about these concepts critically and analytically. Well-written procedures are guaranteed to work. Reproducible data tables teach students how to organize their data so it is easily analyzed. Comprehensive teacher notes include a master materials list, solution preparation guide, complete sample data, and answers to all questions. Detailed lab hints and teaching tips show you how to conduct the experiment in your lab setting and how to identify student errors and misconceptions before students are led astray.

***Chemical demonstrations*** provide another teaching tool for seeing chemistry in action. Because they are both visual and interactive, demonstrations allow teachers to take students on a journey of observation and understanding. Demonstrations provide additional resources to develop central themes and to magnify the power of observation in the classroom. Demonstrations using discrepant events challenge student misconceptions that must be broken down before new concepts can be learned. Use demonstrations to introduce new ideas, illustrate abstract concepts that cannot be covered in lab experiments, and provide a spark of excitement that will capture student interest and attention.

## Safety, flexibility, and choice

Safety always comes first. Depend on Flinn Scientific to give you upfront advice and guidance on all safety and disposal issues. Each activity begins with a description of the hazards involved and the necessary safety precautions to avoid exposure to these hazards. Additional safety, handling, and disposal information is also contained in the teacher notes.

The selection of experiments and demonstrations in each Flinn ChemTopic™ Labs manual gives you the flexibility to choose activities that match the concepts your students need to learn. No single teacher will do all of the experiments and demonstrations with a single class. Some experiments and demonstrations may be more helpful with a beginning-level class, while others may be more suitable with an honors class. All of the experiments and demonstrations have been keyed to national content standards in science education.

## Chemistry is an experimental science!

Whether they are practicing key measurement skills or searching for trends in the chemical properties of substances, all students will benefit from the opportunity to discover chemistry by doing chemistry. No matter what chemistry textbook you use in the classroom, Flinn ChemTopic™ Labs will help you give your students the necessary knowledge, skills, attitudes, and values to be successful in chemistry.

# About the Curriculum Advisory Board

Flinn Scientific is honored to work with an outstanding group of dedicated chemistry teachers. The members of the Flinn ChemTopic Labs Advisory Board have generously contributed their proven experiments, demonstrations, and teaching tips to create these topic lab manuals. The wisdom, experience, creativity, and insight reflected in their lab activities guarantee that students who perform them will be more successful in learning chemistry. On behalf of all chemistry teachers, we thank the Advisory Board members for their service to the teaching profession and their dedication to the field of chemistry education.

**Bob Becker** teaches chemistry and AP chemistry at Kirkwood High School in Kirkwood, MO. Bob received his B.A. from Yale University and M.Ed. from Washington University and has 16 years of teaching experience. A well-known demonstrator, Bob has conducted more than 100 demonstration workshops across the U.S. and Canada and is currently a Team Leader for the Flinn Foundation Summer Workshop Program. His creative and unusual demonstrations have been published in the *Journal of Chemical Education,* the *Science Teacher,* and *Chem13 News*. Bob is the author of two books of chemical demonstrations, *Twenty Demonstrations Guaranteed to Knock Your Socks Off, Volumes I and II,* published by Flinn Scientific. Bob has been awarded the James Bryant Conant Award in High School Teaching from the American Chemical Society, the Regional Catalyst Award from the Chemical Manufacturers Association, and the Tandy Technology Scholar Award.

**Kathleen J. Dombrink** teaches chemistry and advanced-credit college chemistry at McCluer North High School in Florissant, MO. Kathleen received her B.A. in Chemistry from Holy Names College and M.S. in Chemistry from St. Louis University and has more than 31 years of teaching experience. Recognized for her strong support of professional development, Kathleen has been selected to participate in the Fulbright Memorial Fund Teacher Program in Japan and NEWMAST and Dow/NSTA Workshops. She served as co-editor of the inaugural issues of *Chem Matters* and was a Woodrow Wilson National Fellowship Foundation Chemistry Team Member for more than 11 years. Kathleen is currently a Team Leader for the Flinn Foundation Summer Workshop Program. Kathleen has received the Presidential Award, the Midwest Regional Teaching Award from the American Chemical Society, the Tandy Technology Scholar Award, and a Regional Catalyst Award from the Chemical Manufacturers Association.

**Robert Lewis** teaches chemistry and AP chemistry at Downers Grove North High School in Downers Grove, IL. Robert received his B.A. from North Central College and M.A. from University of the South and has more than 26 years of teaching experience. He was a founding member of Weird Science, a group of chemistry teachers that has traveled throughout the country to stimulate teacher interest and enthusiasm for using demonstrations to teach science. Robert was a Chemistry Team Leader for the Woodrow Wilson National Fellowship Foundation and is currently a Team Leader for the Flinn Foundation Summer Workshop Program. Robert has received the Presidential Award, the James Bryant Conant Award in High School Teaching from the American Chemical Society, the Tandy Technology Scholar Award, a Regional Catalyst Award from the Chemical Manufacturers Association, and a Golden Apple Award from the State of Illinois.

**John G. Little** teaches chemistry and AP chemistry at St. Mary's High School in Stockton, CA. John received his B.S. and M.S. in Chemistry from University of the Pacific and has more than 36 years of teaching experience. Highly respected for his well-designed labs, John is the author of two lab manuals, *Chemistry Microscale Laboratory Manual* (D. C. Heath), and *Microscale Experiments for General Chemistry* (with Kenneth Williamson, Houghton Mifflin). He is also a contributing author to *Science Explorer* (Prentice Hall) and *World of Chemistry* (McDougal Littell). John served as a Chemistry Team Leader for the Woodrow Wilson National Fellowship Foundation from 1988 to 1997 and is currently a Team Leader for the Flinn Foundation Summer Workshop Program. He has been recognized for his dedicated teaching with the Tandy Technology Scholar Award and the Regional Catalyst Award from the Chemical Manufacturers Association.

**Lee Marek** retired from teaching chemistry at Naperville North High School in Naperville, IL and currently works at the University of Illinois—Chicago. Lee received his B.S. in Chemical Engineering from the University of Illinois and M.S. degrees in both Physics and Chemistry from Roosevelt University. He has more than 31 years of teaching experience and is currently a Team Leader for the Flinn Foundation Summer Workshop Program. His students have won national recognition in the International Chemistry Olympiad, the Westinghouse Science Talent Search, and the Internet Science and Technology Fair. Lee was also a founding member of Weird Science and has presented more than 500 demonstration and teaching workshops for more than 300,000 students and teachers across the country. Lee has performed science demonstrations on the *David Letterman Show* 20 times. Lee has received the Presidential Award, the James Bryant Conant Award in High School Teaching from the American Chemical Society, the National Catalyst Award from the Chemical Manufacturers Association, and the Tandy Technology Scholar Award.

**John Mauch** teaches chemistry and AP chemistry at Braintree High School in Braintree, MA. John received his B.A. in Chemistry from Whitworth College and M.A. in Curriculum and Education from Washington State University and has 26 years of teaching experience. John is an expert in microscale chemistry and is the author of two lab manuals, *Chemistry in Microscale, Volumes I and II* (Kendall/Hunt). He is also a dynamic and prolific demonstrator and workshop leader. John has presented the Flinn Scientific Chem Demo Extravaganza show at NSTA conventions for eight years and has conducted more than 100 workshops across the country. John was a Chemistry Team Member for the Woodrow Wilson National Fellowship Foundation program for four years and is currently a Board Member for the Flinn Foundation Summer Workshop Program. John has received the Massachusetts Chemistry Teacher of the Year Award from the New England Institute of Chemists.

**Dave Tanis** is Associate Professor of Chemistry at Grand Valley State University in Allendale, MI. Dave received his B.S. in Physics and Mathematics from Calvin College and M.S. in Chemistry from Case Western Reserve University. He taught high school chemistry for 26 years before joining the staff at Grand Valley State University to direct a coalition for improving pre-college math and science education. Dave later joined the faculty at Grand Valley State University and currently teaches courses for pre-service teachers. The author of two laboratory manuals, Dave acknowledges the influence of early encounters with Hubert Alyea, Marge Gardner, Henry Heikkinen, and Bassam Shakhashiri in stimulating his long-standing interest in chemical demonstrations and experiments. Continuing this tradition of mentorship, Dave has led more than 40 one-week institutes for chemistry teachers and served as a Team Member for the Woodrow Wilson National Fellowship Foundation for 13 years. He is currently a Board Member for the Flinn Foundation Summer Workshop Program. Dave received the College Science Teacher of the Year Award from the Michigan Science Teachers Association.

# Preface
## Chemistry of Gases

The historical foundation of modern chemistry was built on an understanding of the chemistry of gases. Studies of hydrogen and oxygen in the 18th century led to the modern definition of an element versus a compound and revealed what happens in a chemical reaction. From these historical roots, the study of gases continues to influence both science and society. As we learn more about the role of greenhouse gases in the chemistry of the atmosphere, the chemistry of gases remains a vital area of research in the 21st century as well. The purpose of *Chemistry of Gases,* Volume 8 in the Flinn ChemTopic™ Labs series, is to provide high school chemistry teachers with laboratory activities that will help students investigate the preparation and properties of the common gases. Four experiments and six demonstrations illustrate a variety of techniques for the preparation of gases and reveal the unique physical and chemical properties of common gases.

### Common Gases

Pure substances, whether solid, liquid or gas, have a constant composition and characteristic physical and chemical properties. In "Common Gases," students prepare five common gases and study the properties that make them unique. Which gases are lighter than air? Which gases have an odor? Use this introductory level experiment to review physical and chemical properties of substances or to provide experience in writing and balancing chemical equations. This survey experiment is also well-suited for use in an applications-oriented chemistry course.

### Macroscale and Microscale Techniques

In "Collecting Gases by Water Displacement," a demonstration procedure, students observe the principle of collecting a gas by water displacement. The large-scale procedure is reduced to a safer and more convenient level in the microscale experiment "Preparing and Testing Hydrogen Gas." Students prepare hydrogen gas and study its density and combustion reaction with air. The microscale adaptation is fast and safe, making it possible for students to repeat the experiment several times as they study the variables that affect the combustion of hydrogen. Supplementary instructions are also provided for the preparation of oxygen gas. The innovative "gas in a syringe" method for preparing gases is featured in two additional microscale experiments. In "Oxygen, What a Flame," students prepare oxygen gas and investigate its role in combustion and oxidation–reduction reactions. In "Carbon Dioxide, What a Gas," students perform classic tests to analyze this important gas and learn about its acid–base properties.

### Exciting Demonstrations

Five demonstrations allow the high school chemistry teacher to showcase in colorful and dramatic fashion the physical and chemical properties of a variety of gases. Acid–base indicators in "Solubility of Carbon Dioxide" and "Solubility of Ammonia" provide a rainbow of color changes to compare the solubility of these gases and to contrast their acidic and basic properties, respectively. The acidic nature of carbon dioxide is also featured in "The Collapsing Bottle" demonstration, where the exothermic reaction of carbon dioxide with sodium hydroxide in a soda bottle results in the bottle collapsing in on itself. "Underwater Fireworks" provides a rather spectacular demonstration of the energy released when bubbles of chlorine and acetylene gas collide under water and react. The density of hydrocarbon vapors and their flammability are illustrated in the "Flaming Vapor Ramp" demonstration. Use this demonstration to underscore the importance of fire safety rules, not only in the lab but in the home as well.

### Safety, Flexibility, and Choice

The overlapping selection of experiments and demonstrations in *Chemistry of Gases* gives you the ability to cover the topics you feel are important in the safest, most effective manner possible. Depend on Flinn Scientific to give you the information and resources to work safely with your students and to help them succeed. Your students will benefit as they learn to appreciate the historical role of the study of gases and to recognize its continuing role in the development of chemistry as the central science. All of the experiments and demonstrations in the *Chemistry of Gases* have been thoroughly tested and retested. You know they will work! Use the experiment summaries and concepts on the following pages to locate the concepts you want to teach and to choose activities that will help you meet your goals.

# Format and Features

## Flinn ChemTopic™ Labs

All experiments and demonstrations in Flinn ChemTopic™ Labs are printed in a $10\frac{7}{8}" \times 11"$ format with a wide 2" margin on the inside of each page. This reduces the printed area of each page to a standard $8\frac{1}{2}" \times 11"$ format suitable for copying.

The wide margin assures you the entire printed area can be easily reproduced without damaging the binding. The margin also provides a convenient place for teachers to add their own notes.

**Concepts** — Use these bulleted lists along with state and local standards, lesson plans, and your textbook to identify activities that will allow you to accomplish specific learning goals and objectives.

**Background** — A balanced source of information for students to understand why they are doing an experiment, what they are doing, and the types of questions the activity is designed to answer. This section is not meant to be exhaustive or to replace the students' textbook, but rather to identify the core concepts that should be covered before starting the lab.

**Experiment Overview** — Clearly defines the purpose of each experiment and how students will achieve this goal. Performing an experiment without a purpose is like getting travel directions without knowing your destination. It doesn't work, especially if you run into a roadblock and need to take a detour!

**Pre-Lab Questions** — Making sure that students are prepared for lab is the single most important element of lab safety. Pre-lab questions introduce new ideas or concepts, review key calculations, and reinforce safety recommendations. The pre-lab questions may be assigned as homework in preparation for lab or they may be used as the basis of a cooperative class activity before lab.

**Materials** — Lists chemical names, formulas, and amounts for all reagents—along with specific glassware and equipment—needed to perform the experiment as written. The material dispensing area is a main source of student delay, congestion, and accidents. Three dispensing stations per room are optimum for a class of 24 students working in pairs. To safely substitute different items for any of the recommended materials, refer to the *Lab Hints* section in each experiment or demonstration.

**Safety Precautions** — Instruct and warn students of the hazards associated with the materials or procedure and give specific recommendations and precautions to protect students from these hazards. Please review this section with students before beginning each experiment.

**Procedure** — This section contains a stepwise, easy-to-follow procedure, where each step generally refers to one action item. Contains reminders about safety and recording data where appropriate. For inquiry-based experiments the procedure may restate the experiment objective and give general guidelines for accomplishing this goal.

**Data Tables** — Data tables are included for each experiment and are referred to in the procedure. These are provided for convenience and to teach students the importance of keeping their data organized in order to analyze it. To encourage more student involvement, many teachers prefer to have students prepare their own data tables. This is an excellent pre-lab preparation activity—it ensures that students have read the procedure and are prepared for lab.

**Post-Lab Questions or Data Analysis** — This section takes students step-by-step through what they did, what they observed, and what it means. Meaningful questions encourage analysis and promote critical thinking skills. Where students need to perform calculations or graph data to analyze the results, these steps are also laid out sequentially and in order.

# Format and Features

## Teacher's Notes

**Master Materials List**  
Lists the chemicals, glassware, and equipment needed to perform the experiment. All amounts have been calculated for a class of 30 students working in pairs. For smaller or larger class sizes or different working group sizes, please adjust the amounts proportionately.

**Preparation of Solutions**  
Calculations and procedures are given for preparing all solutions, based on a class size of 30 students working in pairs. With the exception of particularly hazardous materials, the solution amounts generally include 10% extra to account for spillage and waste. Solution volumes may be rounded to convenient glassware sizes (100-mL, 250-mL, 500-mL, etc.).

**Safety Precautions**  
Repeats the safety precautions given to the students and includes more detailed information relating to safety and handling of chemicals and glassware. Refers to Material Safety Data Sheets that should be available for all chemicals used in the laboratory.

**Disposal**  
Refers to the current *Flinn Scientific Catalog/Reference Manual* for general guidelines and specific procedures governing the disposal of laboratory waste. Because we recommend that teachers review local regulations before beginning any disposal procedure, the information given in this section is for general reference purposes only. However, if a disposal step is included as part of the experimental procedure itself, then the specific solutions needed for disposal are described in this section.

**Lab Hints**  
This section reveals common sources of student errors and misconceptions and where students are likely to need help. Identifies the recommended length of time needed to perform each experiment, suggests alternative chemicals and equipment that may be used, and reminds teachers about new techniques (filtration, pipeting, etc.) that should be reviewed prior to lab.

**Teaching Tips**  
This section puts the experiment in perspective so that teachers can judge in more detail how and where a particular experiment will fit into their curriculum. Identifies the working assumptions about what students need to know in order to perform the experiment and answer the questions. Highlights historical background and applications-oriented information that may be of interest to students.

**Sample Data**  
Complete, actual sample data obtained by performing the experiment exactly as written is included for each experiment. Student data will vary.

**Answers to All Questions**  
Representative or typical answers to all questions. Includes sample calculations and graphs for all data analysis questions. Information of special interest to teachers only in this section is identified by the heading "Note to the teacher." Student answers will vary.

Look for these icons in the *Experiment Summaries and Concepts* section and in the *Teacher's Notes* of individual experiments to identify inquiry-, microscale-, and technology-based experiments, respectively.

# Experiment Summaries and Concepts

## Experiment

### Common Gases—Physical and Chemical Properties

Colorless, odorless, tasteless—the physical properties of many gases make them invisible to our senses. But that doesn't mean that all gases are the same. Just like solids and liquids, gases have characteristic physical and chemical properties. Which gases are lighter than air? Which gases are flammable? The purpose of this introductory-level experiment is to prepare five common gases and investigate their physical and chemical properties.

### Preparing and Testing Hydrogen Gas—A Microscale Approach

Hydrogen is the second most abundant element in living things. Despite its abundance, very little hydrogen is found on Earth in its free state as hydrogen gas. This is because hydrogen combines readily with other elements. What properties of hydrogen gas make it unique? How can hydrogen gas be prepared in the lab? In this microscale experiment, students collect hydrogen gas by water displacement and study its density and combustion.

### Oxygen, What a Flame—Microscale Gas Chemistry

Oxygen gas! Plants make it and we breathe it. Although we live in an atmosphere containing oxygen gas, the element is also a very reactive substance. The role of oxygen in combustion illustrates its great reactivity. The purpose of this experiment is to prepare oxygen gas and observe its characteristic oxidation–reduction and combustion reactions. Students learn a new and creative "gases in a syringe" method for generating gases that can be adapted to many different gases.

### Carbon Dioxide, What a Gas—Microscale Gas Chemistry

Carbon dioxide gas is a product of respiration and combustion. We exhale it with every breath we take. If plants did not consume the excess carbon dioxide during photosynthesis, we would soon die from the toxic levels of carbon dioxide in the atmosphere. In this microscale experiment, students prepare carbon dioxide gas in a syringe and study its properties. Students learn about the acid–base properties of carbon dioxide as they perform classic tests to analyze this important gas.

## Concepts

- Physical property
- Chemical property

- Hydrogen gas
- Physical properties
- Chemical properties
- Flammability

- Gas generation
- Oxygen gas
- Combustion
- Oxidation–reduction

- Preparation of gases
- Carbon dioxide gas
- Combustion
- Acid–base reactions

# Experiment Summaries and Concepts

## Demonstration

### Concepts

*Collecting Gases by Water Displacement—Demonstration Procedure*

Gas generator bottles provide an easy way to generate and collect gas samples for demonstration purposes. Specific instructions are included for generating hydrogen gas and collecting the gas by water displacement.

- Generation of gases
- Water displacement
- Hydrogen gas

*Underwater Fireworks—Chemical Demonstration*

Every day can be the 4th of July with this exciting demonstration. Chlorine and acetylene gas are bubbled into the bottom of a large graduated cylinder filled with water. As the bubbles collide, the two gases react to produce instantaneous, bright flashes of light.

- Chlorine gas
- Acetylene gas
- Chemical properties

*Flaming Vapor Ramp—Safety Demonstration*

Vapors from a volatile, flammable liquid are heavier than air and can travel along a countertop to an ignition source. Their flames will quickly follow the vapor trail back to the source and may result in a large fire or explosion. Illustrate the importance of fire safety rules with this safe demonstration of the density and flammability of hydrocarbon vapors.

- Density of gases
- Flammability
- Fire safety

*The Collapsing Bottle—A Carbon Dioxide Demonstration*

Can an invisible gas cause a two-liter plastic soda bottle to suddenly collapse in on itself? Fill a plastic soda bottle with carbon dioxide gas and add sodium hydroxide solution. Observe as the bottle gets hot and then collapses as it is crushed inward by the force of atmospheric pressure.

- Carbon dioxide gas
- Acid–base reactions
- Atmospheric pressure

*Solubility of Carbon Dioxide—Dry Ice Color Show*

Add a small piece of dry ice to a series of colored indicator solutions and watch as the solutions immediately begin to "boil" and change color. Teach students about sublimation and the acid–base properties of dry ice with this colorful and "cool" demonstration.

- Carbon dioxide gas
- Sublimation
- Acid–base indicators

*Solubility of Ammonia—Indicator Color Show*

Teach students about gas solubility and the acid–base properties of ammonia gas with this indicator color show. Ammonia gas is collected in jumbo pipet bulbs and a drop of indicator solution is drawn into each pipet bulb. The ammonia gas instantly dissolves and the bulb immediately fills with a different color indicator solution.

- Ammonia gas
- Gas solubility
- Acid–base indicators

Teacher Notes

# Common Gases
## Physical and Chemical Properties

### Introduction

It's easy to overlook the chemistry of gases—because many gases are colorless and odorless, we may not notice them. If we reflect on the environmental impact of different gases in the atmosphere, however, we realize that not all gases are the same. Just like solids and liquids, all gases have characteristic physical and chemical properties. Let's look at the properties of some common gases.

### Concepts

- Physical property
- Chemical property

### Background

Pure substances, whether solid or liquid or gas, have a constant composition or chemical makeup. Solid copper metal (Cu), liquid water ($H_2O$), and gaseous carbon dioxide ($CO_2$) are examples of pure substances. Pure substances have characteristic physical and chemical properties that can be used to describe and analyze them. A physical property is a characteristic of matter that can be observed or measured without changing the chemical composition. Examples of physical properties include color, odor, physical state (at room temperature), conductivity, melting point, boiling point, and solubility. A chemical property describes the ability of a substance to undergo changes in its chemical composition. Examples of chemical properties include flammability, acidity, and corrosion.

#### Experiment Overview

The purpose of this experiment is to prepare five common gases and observe their physical and chemical properties.

### Pre-Lab Questions

1. Read the entire *Procedure* and the accompanying *Safety Precautions*. What hazards are associated with the use of nitric acid?

2. What is the proper procedure for smelling a chemical in the lab?

3. Complete the following balanced equations for the reactions in test tubes A–E. Enter the name and formula of each gas in the data table.

    (a) $NaHCO_3(aq) + HCl(aq) \rightarrow NaCl(aq) + H_2O(l) + \underline{\quad}$ (g)

    (b) $Cu(s) + 4HNO_3(aq) \rightarrow Cu(NO_3)_2(aq) + 2H_2O(l) + 2\underline{\quad}$ (g)

    (c) $NH_4Cl(aq) + NaOH(aq) \rightarrow NaCl(aq) + H_2O(l) + \underline{\quad}$ (g)

    (d) $2H_2O_2(aq) \rightarrow 2H_2O(l) + \underline{\quad}$ (g)

    *Note:* The catalyst ($MnO_2$) is not represented in the balanced chemical equation.

    (e) $Mg(s) + 2HCl(aq) \rightarrow MgCl_2(aq) + \underline{\quad}$ (g)

*This is a survey experiment to compare the properties of different gases. See individual experiments in this book for generating and collecting hydrogen, oxygen, and carbon dioxide.*

Common Gases

# Common Gases – Page 2

## Materials

| | |
|---|---|
| Ammonium chloride, $NH_4Cl$, 0.1 g | Forceps |
| Copper foil, Cu, 5-mm square | Graduated cylinder, 10-mL |
| Hydrogen peroxide, $H_2O_2$, 3%, 5 mL | Litmus paper, 1 piece |
| Hydrochloric acid, HCl, 3 M, 7 mL | Matches |
| Magnesium ribbon, Mg, 2-cm strip | Parafilm®, 3-cm square piece |
| Manganese dioxide, $MnO_2$, 0.1 g | Spatula |
| Nitric acid, $HNO_3$, 6 M, 1 mL | Stirring rod |
| Sodium bicarbonate solution, $NaHCO_3$, 0.1 M, 2 mL | Test tubes, medium, 5 |
| Sodium hydroxide solution, NaOH, 3 M, 1 mL | Test tube rack |
| Water, distilled or deionized | Wash bottle |
| Beaker, 150-mL | Wood splints, 3 |

## Safety Precautions

*Nitric acid is severely corrosive and a strong oxidizing agent. Work with nitric acid in a fume hood only and do not remove from the hood. Hydrochloric acid is toxic by ingestion or inhalation and is corrosive to skin and eyes. Sodium hydroxide is a corrosive liquid and is especially dangerous to the eyes. Notify your teacher and clean up all spills immediately. Hydrogen peroxide is a skin and eye irritant. Avoid contact of all chemicals with eyes and skin. Copper foil edges are sharp and may cause cuts; handle with care or use forceps. Wear chemical splash goggles and chemical-resistant gloves and apron. Wash hands thoroughly with soap and water before leaving the lab. Never sniff any substance in the chemical laboratory—to detect the odor of a substance, place the open container about 6 inches away from the nose and use your hand to waft the vapors toward the nose.*

## Procedure

1. Label five medium test tubes A–E and place them in a test tube rack.

2. Pour 2 mL of 0.1 M sodium bicarbonate into test tube A.

3. Add 2 mL of 3 M hydrochloric acid into test tube A and observe the color and odor of the gas. Record the observations in the data table. *Note:* If the gas has no color or odor, write colorless or odorless, respectively.

4. Light a wooden splint and insert the burning splint well down into the test tube (but NOT into the liquid). Record the observations in the data table.

5. Bring test tube B to the fume hood and carefully add 1 mL of nitric acid to the test tube.

6. Place test tube B in a rack in the fume hood and add one small piece of copper foil. Observe and record the color of the gas in the data table. *Caution:* Do NOT attempt to smell the odor of the gas! Leave the test tube in the fume hood.

7. Add a small amount (about a spatula-full, approximately 0.1 g) of solid ammonium chloride to test tube C, followed by 5 mL of water. Stir to dissolve the solid.

8. Place the test tube in a 150-mL beaker containing about 75 mL of hot tap water.

---

Teacher Notes

*The reaction of copper metal with 6 M nitric acid is relatively slow. The solution turns blue-green within three minutes, and a brown gas is observed after five minutes. Place a piece of white paper behind the test tube to observe the color of the gas. The preparation of $NO_2$ may be done as a teacher-led demonstration, if desired.*

**Teacher Notes**

9. Add 10 drops of 3 M sodium hydroxide to test tube C. Gently swirl the test tube to mix the contents and cautiously observe the odor. Record the color and odor of the gas in the data table. *Caution:* To observe the odor, hold the test tube about 6–8 inches away from the nose and use your hand to waft the vapors toward you. Do NOT "sniff" the odor of any chemical in the laboratory.

10. Moisten a strip of litmus paper with a drop of distilled water and place the moistened litmus paper on top of test tube C. Record the color of the litmus paper in the data table.

11. Pour 5 mL of 3% hydrogen peroxide solution into test tube D.

12. Add a small amount (about the size of a grain of rice) of manganese dioxide to test tube D and gently swirl the test tube to initiate the reaction. Observe and record the color and odor of the gas in the data table.

13. Seal the mouth of test tube D by stretching a piece of Parafilm® over the top of the tube. Allow the test tube to sit undisturbed for 1–2 minutes.

14. Prepare a burning wood splint.

15. Remove the Parafilm from the test tube. Quickly blow out the splint so that it is glowing rather than burning. Insert the glowing splint down into the test tube almost to the liquid, then bring it out. Record your observations in the data table.

16. Carefully add 5 mL of 3 M hydrochloric acid to test tube E.

17. Strike a match, carfully add one piece of magnesium ribbon into the acid in test tube E, and quickly place the lighted match directly above the mouth of the test tube. Record your observations, including the color and odor of the gas, in the data table.

18. Dispose of the contents of test tubes A–E as directed by your instructor.

*As noted, step 17 must be done quickly to observe the characteristic "pop" test for hydrogen gas. Hydrochloric acid is in excess in the test tube. If students fail to observe the hydrogen reaction the first time, have them try again with a fresh piece of magnesium ribbon.*

**Common Gases** – Page 4

Name: _____

Class/Lab Period: _____

# Common Gases

## Data Table

| | Physical and Chemical Properties of Common Gases | |
|---|---|---|
| Test Tube A | Name and Formula of Gas | |
| | Color and Odor | |
| | Burning Splint Test | |
| Test Tube B | Name and Formula of Gas | |
| | Color | |
| Test Tube C | Name and Formula of Gas | |
| | Color and Odor | |
| | Litmus Test | |
| Test Tube D | Name and Formula of Gas | |
| | Color and Odor | |
| | Glowing Splint Test | |
| Test Tube E | Name and Formula of Gas | |
| | Color and Odor | |
| | Match Test | |

Teacher Notes

Teacher Notes

**Post-Lab Questions**

1. Identify the common gas or gases prepared in this experiment:

    (a) Contributes to industrial smog and air pollution? _____

    (b) Lightest element in the universe? _____

    (c) Needed for the burning of fossil fuels and for respiration in animals? _____

    (d) Dissolves readily in water and is used as a fertilizer? _____

    (e) Combustible? _____

    (f) Extinguishes a flame? _____

    (g) Has an odor? _____

    (h) Required for photosynthesis? _____

2. Explain the observations of the glowing splint test for oxygen.

3. Explain the observation of the litmus test for ammonia.

4. Circle and label the physical and chemical properties in the following description of chlorine:

    *"Chlorine is a greenish-yellow gas that dissolves in water and is toxic to humans. It combines violently with sodium metal to form sodium chloride, a white solid that melts at 800 °C."*

5. Consult a Periodic Table: Name the elements that exist as gases at room temperature and give their symbols or formulas. *Hint:* Recall that some elements exist as diatomic molecules in their free state.

6. (a) Which gaseous elements (see Question #5) are toxic? (b) Which gaseous elements are considered inert or unreactive?

# Teacher's Notes
## Common Gases

**Master Materials List** *(for a class of 30 students working in pairs)*

Ammonium chloride, $NH_4Cl$, 2 g
Copper foil, Cu, 5-mm squares, 15
Hydrogen peroxide, $H_2O_2$, 3%, 125 mL*
Hydrochloric acid, HCl, 3 M, 100 mL
Magnesium ribbon, Mg, 2-cm strips, 15
Manganese dioxide, $MnO_2$, 2 g
Nitric acid, $HNO_3$, 6 M, 20 mL*
Sodium bicarbonate solution, $NaHCO_3$, 0.1 M, 50 mL
Sodium hydroxide solution, NaOH, 3 M, 25 mL
Water, distilled or deionized
Beakers, 150-mL, 15
Forceps, 15
Graduated cylinders, 10-mL, 15
Litmus paper, 15 pieces
Matches
Parafilm® or plastic film wrap[†]
Spatulas, 15
Stirring rods, 15
Test tubes, 15 × 125 mm, 75
Test tube racks, 15
Wash bottles, 15
Wood splints, 45

*We recommend the purchase of ready-made 6 M nitric acid (Flinn Catalog No. N0049) and 3% hydrogen peroxide (Flinn Catalog No. H0009) solutions.

[†]Parafilm is a thermoplastic, pliable, self-sealing film that can be used to seal almost anything. Cut into 3-cm squares for student use.

## Preparation of Solutions

*Hydrochloric Acid, 3 M:* Carefully add 50 mL of concentrated (12 M) hydrochloric acid to about 100 mL of distilled or deionized water. Stir to mix and allow to cool, then dilute to 200 mL with distilled water. *Note:* Always add acid to water.

*Sodium Bicarbonate, 0.1 M:* Dissolve 0.84 g of sodium bicarbonate in about 50 mL of distilled or deionized water. Mix to dissolve, then dilute to 100 mL with distilled water.

*Sodium Hydroxide, 3 M:* Cool 50 mL of distilled or deionized water in an ice bath and carefully add 12.0 g of sodium hydroxide. Mix to dissolve and allow the solution to come to room temperature, then dilute to 100 mL with distilled water.

## Safety Precautions

*Nitric acid is severely corrosive and a strong oxidizing agent. Work with nitric acid in a fume hood only and do not remove from the hood. Hydrochloric acid is toxic by ingestion or inhalation and is corrosive to skin and eyes. Sodium hydroxide is a corrosive liquid and is especially dangerous to eyes. Keep spill control materials on hand to cleam up chemical spills. Hydrogen peroxide is a skin and eye irritant. Avoid contact of all chemicals with eyes and skin. Copper foil edges are sharp and may cause cuts; handle with care or use forceps. Wear chemical splash goggles and chemical-resistant gloves and apron. Never sniff any substance in the chemical laboratory—to detect the odor of a substance, place the open container about 6 inches away from the nose and use your hand to waft the vapors toward the*

**Teacher Notes**

nose. Please consult current Material Safety Data Sheets for additional safety, handling, and disposal information. Remind students to wash hands thoroughly with soap and water before leaving the lab.

## Disposal

Consult your current *Flinn Scientific Catalog/Reference Manual* for general guidelines and specific procedures governing the disposal of laboratory waste. Excess sodium hydroxide solution may be neutralized with acid and disposed of accordng to Flinn Suggested Disposal Method #10. Excess acid solutions may be neutralized with base and disposed of according to Flinn Suggested Disposal Method #24b. The waste solutions may be flushed down the drain with plenty of excess water according to Flinn Suggested Disposal Method #26b.

## Lab Hints

- The laboratory work for this experiment can easily be completed within a typical 50-minute lab period. The activity is very versatile and can be used in many different places in the chemistry curriculum. Use the experiment to introduce physical and chemical properties, to review the periodic table, to provide experience in writing and balancing chemical equations, or to illustrate the properties of common gases. The experiment is also well-suited to applications-oriented chemistry courses such as *Chemistry in the Community*.

- The reagents for the preparation of nitric acid and hydrogen have been chosen with safety in mind. Although copper metal gives a faster reaction with concentrated nitric acid, using 6 M nitric acid is safer. In addition, the slower reaction allows students to observe the actual changes taking place in the reaction mixture as the reaction proceeds. Remind students not to remove the test tube from the hood.

- Demonstrate the wafting technique to your students and remind them to never sniff a chemical in the laboratory.

## Teaching Tips

- Hydrogen and oxygen may be generated using the reactions shown in this experiment and collected by water displacement if desired. See the experiment "Preparing and Testing Hydrogen Gas" in this volume of the *Flinn ChemTopic™ Labs* series for a suitable microscale procedure.

- Atmospheric chemistry represents an interesting application of chemistry as "the central science." The common gases prepared in this experiment provide a good starting point for studying the chemistry of the atmosphere. Possible topics for discussion include the composition and properties of gases in the atmosphere, the reactions of carbon dioxide that are involved in the carbon cycle, the role of carbon dioxide in global warming, and the reactions of nitrogen dioxide that contribute to air pollution and the loss of the ozone layer.

Common Gases

**Teacher's Notes**

**Answers to Pre-Lab Questions** *(Student answers will vary.)*

1. Read the entire *Procedure* and the accompanying *Safety Precautions*. What hazards are associated with the use of nitric acid?

    *Nitric acid is severely corrosive and a strong oxidizing agent. Work with nitric acid in the fume hood only and do not remove from the hood. Wear chemical splash goggles and chemical-resistant gloves and apron and avoid contact with eyes and skin. Notify the teacher and clean up all spills immediately.*

2. What is the proper procedure for smelling a chemical in the lab?

    *Never sniff any chemical in the lab. To observe the odor of a substance, hold the container about 6 inches away from the nose and use your hand to carefully waft the vapors toward the nose.*

3. Complete the following balanced equations for the reactions in test tubes A–E. Enter the name and formula of each gas in the data table.

    (a) $NaHCO_3(aq) + HCl(aq) \rightarrow NaCl(aq) + H_2O(l) + \mathbf{CO_2(g)}$
    *Carbon dioxide*

    (b) $Cu(s) + 4HNO_3(aq) \rightarrow Cu(NO_3)_2(aq) + 2H_2O(l) + \mathbf{2NO_2(g)}$
    *Nitrogen dioxide*

    (c) $NH_4Cl(aq) + NaOH(aq) \rightarrow NaCl(aq) + H_2O(l) + \mathbf{NH_3(g)}$
    *Ammonia*

    (d) $2H_2O_2(aq) \rightarrow 2H_2O(l) + \mathbf{O_2(g)}$
    *Oxygen*

    (e) $Mg(s) + 2HCl(aq) \rightarrow MgCl_2(aq) + \mathbf{H_2(g)}$
    *Hydrogen*

# Teacher's Notes

Teacher Notes

# Sample Data

*Student data will vary.*

## Data Table

| Physical and Chemical Properties of Common Gases | | |
|---|---|---|
| **Test Tube A** | **Name and Formula of Gas** | Carbon dioxide, $CO_2$ |
| | **Color and Odor** | Colorless and odorless |
| | **Burning Splint Test** | Extinguishes the flame |
| **Test Tube B** | **Name and Formula of Gas** | Nitrogen dioxide, $NO_2$ |
| | **Color** | Brown gas; solution turns blue |
| **Test Tube C** | **Name and Formula of Gas** | Ammonia, $NH_3$ |
| | **Color and Odor** | Colorless; pungent odor |
| | **Litmus Test** | Turns litmus paper blue (basic) |
| **Test Tube D** | **Name and Formula of Gas** | Oxygen, $O_2$ |
| | **Color and Odor** | Colorless; odorless |
| | **Glowing Splint Test** | Spontaneously bursts into flame (reignites) |
| **Test Tube E** | **Name and Formula of Gas** | Hydrogen, $H_2$ |
| | **Color and Odor** | Colorless and odorless |
| | **Match Test** | Soft "pop" and lighted match goes out |

*Why does hydrogen give the characteristic "pop" test? Hydrogen by itself should not react. The slight popping sound occurs as hydrogen escaping from the test tube mixes with oxygen in the air. Eventually a combustible $H_2/O_2$ mixture is produced.*

Common Gases

# Teacher's Notes

**Answers to Post-Lab Questions** *(Student answers will vary.)*

1. Identify the common gas or gases prepared in this experiment:

    (a) Contributes to brown, industrial smog and air pollution? *Nitrogen dioxide*

    (b) Lightest element in the universe? *Hydrogen*

    (c) Needed for the burning of fossil fuels and for respiration in animals? *Oxygen*

    (d) Dissolves readily in water and is used as a fertilizer? *Ammonia*

    (e) Combustible? *Hydrogen*

    (f) Extinguishes a flame? *Carbon dioxide*

    (g) Has an odor? *Ammonia and nitrogen dioxide (The latter is not based on student observation.)*

    (h) Required for photosynthesis? *Carbon dioxide*

2. Explain the observation of the glowing splint test for oxygen.

    *The glowing splint burst into flame because combustion occurs faster in pure oxygen than in air.*

3. Explain the observations of the litmus test for ammonia.

    *Litmus paper turned blue, indicating that ammonia is a basic substance.*

4. Circle and label the physical and chemical properties in the following description of chlorine:

    *"Chlorine is a greenish-yellow gas that dissolves in water and is toxic to humans. It combines violently with sodium metal to form sodium chloride, a white solid that melts at 800 °C."*

    |  | **Physical Properties** | **Chemical Properties** |
    |---|---|---|
    | Chlorine | Greenish-yellow | Toxic to humans |
    |  | Gas | Combines violently with sodium |
    |  | Dissolves in water |  |

5. Consult a Periodic Table: Name the elements that exist as gases at room temperature and give their symbols or formulas. *Hint:* Recall that some elements exist as diatomic molecules in their free state.

    *Hydrogen ($H_2$), helium (He), nitrogen ($N_2$), oxygen ($O_2$), fluorine ($F_2$), neon (Ne), chlorine ($Cl_2$), argon (Ar), krypton (Kr), xenon (Xe), and radon (Rn).*

6. (a) Which gaseous elements (see Question #5) are toxic? (b) Which gaseous elements are considered inert or unreactive?

    (a) *The halogens (fluorine and chlorine) are toxic. Radon is a radiation hazard.*

    (b) *The Noble Gases (helium, neon, argon, krypton, xenon, and radon) are considered inert or unreactive.* **Note to teachers:** *Under extreme conditions, krypton and xenon will react to form compounds of the type $KrF_2$ and $XeO_3$.*

*A good "rule of thumb" for students to learn—all colored gases are toxic!*

*Teacher Notes*

# Preparing and Testing Hydrogen Gas
## A Microscale Approach

## Introduction

Hydrogen is the most abundant element in the universe and the second most abundant element in living things. Despite its abundance, very little hydrogen is found on Earth in the free state as hydrogen gas. This is because hydrogen is easily oxidized and combines readily with many other elements, including carbon, oxygen, and nitrogen. How can hydrogen gas be prepared in the lab?

## Concepts

- Hydrogen gas
- Physical properties
- Chemical properties
- Flammability

## Background

Hydrogen gas was first studied in 1766 by Henry Cavendish, who isolated the "inflammable air" produced in the reaction of metals with acids. The true chemical nature of this gas was not understood until about 20 years later, when Lavoisier correctly explained the reaction that occurs when the gas combines with oxygen to make water. Lavoisier named the gas "hydrogen" from the Greek words meaning "water-former." Most of the hydrogen on Earth is found in water and in petroleum-based products (oil and gas). Hydrogen gas is also the most abundant element in the universe—it is the "fuel" that makes our sun and stars burn brightly.

### Experiment Overview

The purpose of this experiment is to collect hydrogen gas by water displacement and study its properties. Hydrogen gas will be generated by the reaction of zinc metal with hydrochloric acid.

*The historical names of the pure gases—inflammable air ($H_2$), fixed air ($CO_2$), and dephlogisticated air ($O_2$)—reveal much about early theories of chemistry. Lavoisier's explanation of the reaction between hydrogen and oxygen to make water was used to assert that water was not an element—an important conclusion at the time.*

## Pre-Lab Questions

1. Read the *Procedure* section and the accompanying *Safety Precautions*. What hazards are associated with the use of hydrochloric acid?

2. Write a balanced chemical equation for the reaction of zinc metal with hydrochloric acid.

3. What are the two major gases in air? Which one will probably react with hydrogen in the "Test for Mixture of Air and Hydrogen Gas?" What is the likely product of this reaction?

## Materials

| | |
|---|---|
| Hydrochloric acid, HCl, 3 M, 20 mL | Bunsen burner |
| Zinc, granular, Zn, 1 g | Gas-delivery stopper, size 00 |
| Soap solution, 2 mL | Plastic cup, 10-oz |
| Bar straw | Test tube, small |
| Beral-type pipet bulbs, 2 | Toothpicks, wood, 3 |

**Preparing and Testing Hydrogen Gas** – *Page 2*

## Safety Precautions

*Zinc dust may be flammable. Hydrochloric acid is toxic by ingestion and inhalation and is severely corrosive to skin and eyes. Notify your teacher and clean up all acid spills immediately. Hydrogen gas is flammable. Avoid contact of all chemicals with eyes and skin. Wear chemical splash goggles and chemical-resistant gloves and apron. Wash hands thoroughly with soap and water before leaving the laboratory.*

## Procedure

1. Place about 0.5 grams of granular zinc into a small test tube and insert the gas-delivery stopper (see Figure 1).

2. Fill a pipet bulb with water so that the hydrogen gas can be collected by the displacement of water.

3. Set up the gas generator as shown in Figure 2. To generate the hydrogen gas, remove the gas-delivery stopper, fill the test tube about ⅘ full with 3 M hydrochloric acid, and replace the stopper. There should be only a small air space between the acid and the bottom of the stopper. This will reduce the time needed to flush the air out of the gas generator.

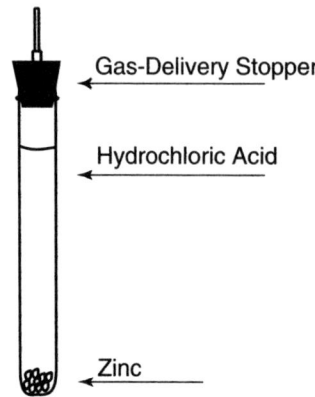

**Figure 1.** Gas-generating unit

4. Place the pipet-bulb full of water on top of the gas-delivery stopper to collect the hydrogen gas by water displacement (see Figure 2).

5. Collect a pipet-bulb full of the gas.

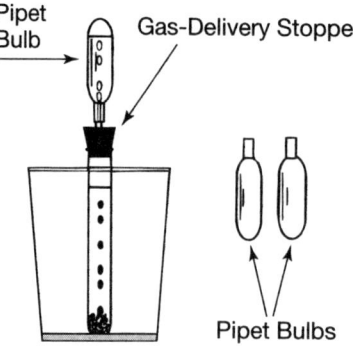

**Figure 2.** Collecting the gas

### Test for Pure Hydrogen Gas

6. To test for pure hydrogen gas, bring a pipet-bulb full of the gas to a Bunsen burner, mouth down. Holding the pipet bulb *horizontally,* place a flaming toothpick near the mouth of the pipet bulb and quickly squeeze the bulb of gas. Record your observations in the data table.

### Test for Mixture of Air and Hydrogen Gas

7. Fill a pipet bulb about ¼ full of water. Collect enough hydrogen gas to displace the water in the bulb.

8. To test the hydrogen–air mixture, bring the pipet bulb to a Bunsen burner, mouth down. Holding the pipet bulb horizontally, place a flaming toothpick near the mouth of the pipet bulb and quickly squeeze the bulb of gas. Record your observations in the data table.

Teacher Notes

*Students may enjoy testing different ratios of air and hydrogen gas in steps 7 and 8. Which mixture produces the largest explosion?*

Flinn ChemTopic™ Labs — Chemistry of Gases

*Page 3 –* **Preparing and Testing Hydrogen Gas**

Teacher Notes

*Relative Density of Hydrogen Gas*

9. Insert a bar straw so that it telescopes into the gas-delivery stopper of the gas-generator unit (see Figure 3).

10. While the hydrogen gas is being generated, place a film of soap solution (using your finger) at the mouth of the straw so that a bubble of hydrogen gas can be formed.

11. When the bubble is approximately 1 cm in diameter, raise the apparatus just above your head and gently blow upward at the bubble in order to jar the bubble loose without breaking it. Record your observations in the data table.

12. Dispose of the test tube contents as directed by your instructor.

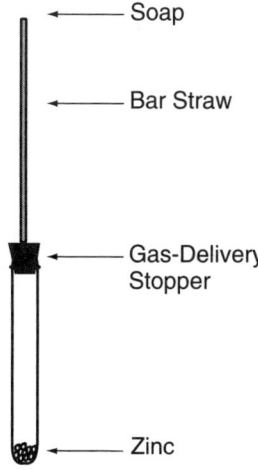

**Figure 3.**

*Bar straws commonly used to mix and stir drinks are recommended for this activity. Regular drinking straws will probably not fit into the one-hole rubber stoppers.*

Preparing and Testing Hydrogen Gas – Page 4

Name: _____

Class/Lab Period: _____

# Preparing and Testing Hydrogen Gas

## Data Table

|  |  |
|---|---|
| Test for Pure Hydrogen Gas |  |
| Test for Mixture of Air and Hydrogen Gas |  |
| Relative Density of Hydrogen Gas |  |

## Post-Lab Questions

1. Is hydrogen gas lighter or heavier than air? Explain based on your observations.

2. Compare the observations made when pure hydrogen was tested versus when a mixture of hydrogen and air was tested.

    (a) Which reaction was more explosive? Why?

    (b) Write a balanced chemical equation for the reaction of hydrogen and oxygen.

Teacher Notes

Flinn ChemTopic™ Labs — Chemistry of Gases

*Page 5 – **Preparing and Testing Hydrogen Gas***

Teacher Notes

3. Summarize the physical and chemical properties of hydrogen gas by indicating whether the following statements are True or False:

   (a) Hydrogen gas is colorless. _____

   (b) Hydrogen does not diffuse in air. _____

   (c) Hydrogen is very soluble in water. _____

   (d) Hydrogen has a greater density than air. _____

   (e) Hydrogen is flammable. _____

   (f) Hydrogen supports combustion. _____

   (g) Hydrogen and air will explode when ignited. _____

4. The reaction of metals with acids is a general reaction that works with a wide variety of different metals and mineral acids. Write balanced chemical equations for the reactions of:

   (a) Zinc with sulfuric acid.

   (b) Aluminum with hydrochloric acid.

# Teacher's Notes
## Preparing and Testing Hydrogen Gas

### Master Materials List

Zinc, granular, Zn, 15 g
Hydrochloric acid, HCl, 3 M, 300 mL
Soap solution, 30 mL
Bar straws, 15
Beral-type pipets, graduated, 30
Bunsen burners, 15

Gas-delivery stoppers, size 00, 15
Plastic cups, 10-oz, 15
Razor blade or scissors
Test tubes, 13 × 100 mm, 15
Toothpicks, wood, 45

### Preparation of Solutions

*Hydrochloric Acid, 3 M:* Carefully add 125 mL of concentrated (12 M) hydrochloric acid to about 200 mL of distilled or deionized water. Stir to mix and allow to cool, then dilute to 500 mL with water. *Note:* Always add acid to water.

### Safety Precautions

*Zinc dust may be flammable. Hydrochloric acid is toxic by ingestion and inhalation and is severely corrosive to skin and eyes. Keep sodium bicarbonate on hand to clean up acid spills. Hydrogen gas is flammable. Wear chemical splash goggles, chemical-resistant gloves, and a chemical-resistant apron. Remind students to wash their hands thoroughly with soap and water before leaving the laboratory. Please consult current Material Safety Data Sheets for additional safety, handling, and disposal information.*

### Disposal

Consult your current *Flinn Scientific Catalog/Reference Manual* for general guidelines and specific procedures governing the disposal of laboratory waste. Excess hydrochloric acid may be neutralized and disposed of according to Flinn Suggested Disposal Method #24b. Zinc metal may be reused or disposed of according to Flinn Suggested Disposal Method #26a. The acidic zinc chloride solutions remaining in the gas generator tubes after this experiment is complete may be neutralized with base and disposed of according to Flinn Suggested Disposal Method #24b.

### Lab Hints

- The pipet bulb used for collecting gases is made by cutting off most of the stem from a graduated Beral pipet (see Figure 4). *Note:* Use a sharp razor blade or scissors to give uniform cuts.

- The remaining portion of the stem from the graduated pipet is then used to make the gas-delivery stopper. Simply cut off a portion of the tip of the graduated stem (see Figure 1) and insert it into a 1-hole rubber stopper. Make extra stoppers and save them for future use.

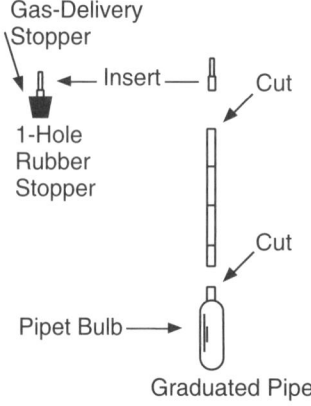

**Figure 4.**

*Save valuable time and money by purchasing ready-made hydrochloric acid solution. See the Master Materials Guide at the back of this book.*

Flinn ChemTopic™ Labs — Chemistry of Gases

Teacher Notes

- The gas-generating unit can be replenished with fresh acid without much loss of time. Remember, when filling the test tube with the acid, fill it about ⅘ full. This will leave only a small volume of air that must be flushed out of the generator before the hydrogen gas is collected.

- The pipet bulb can be removed anytime. Due to the surface tension of water, the pipet bulb can be held upside-down and any water in the bulb will remain there. This bulb can be placed, upside-down, into one of the wells of a 96-well reaction plate. To save time, many pipet bulbs of gas can be collected and placed into the wells of the reaction plate if a small amount of water is left at the neck of the pipet bulb. The water will serve as a seal between the gas and the atmosphere.

## Teaching Tips

- See the *Supplementary Information* section for a complementary microscale procedure for preparing and testing oxygen gas.

- Testing the mixture of hydorgen and air may be extended to determine the optimum mole (volume) ratio of hydrogen and oxygen for combustion. The experiment "Micro Mole Rockets" in *Molar Relationships and Stoichiometry,* Volume 7 in the *Flinn ChemTopic™ Labs* series, is a microscale lab activity in which students measure the explosiveness of the reaction between hydrogen and oxygen. Students generate hydrogen and oxygen gases using the same procedure described in this experiment, and test their combustion properties in mixtures of various proportions.

## Answers to Pre-Lab Questions *(Student answers will vary.)*

1. Read the *Procedure* section and the accompanying *Safety Precautions*. What hazards are associated with the use of hydrochloric acid?

   *Hydrochloric acid is toxic by ingestion and inhalation and is severely corrosive to skin and eyes.*

2. Write a balanced chemical equation for the reaction of zinc metal with hydrochloric acid.

   $Zn(s) + 2HCl(aq) \rightarrow ZnCl_2(aq) + H_2(g)$

3. What are the two major gases in air? Which one will probably react with hydrogen in the "Test for Mixture of Air and Hydrogen Gas?" What is the likely product of this reaction?

   *The two major gases in air are nitrogen (78%) and oxygen (21%). Hydrogen reacts with oxygen in air to produce water.* **Note to teachers:** *A catalyst is needed for the reaction of hydrogen and nitrogen to make ammonia.*

# Teacher's Notes

## Sample Data

*Student data will vary.*

### Data Table

| Properties of Hydrogen Gas | Observations |
|---|---|
| Test for Pure Hydrogen Gas | The flame went out and a soft popping sound was heard. |
| Test for Mixture of Air and Hydrogen Gas | The flame went out and a loud popping sound was heard. There was a recoil effect—the pipet bulb was pushed back by the force of the mini-explosion. |
| Relative Density of Hydrogen Gas | The hydrogen-filled soap bubble rose and floated in the air. |

## Answers to Post-Lab Questions *(Student answers will vary.)*

1. Is hydrogen gas lighter or heavier than air? Explain based on your observations.

    *Hydrogen gas is lighter than air—it rises and floats in the air.*

2. Compare the observations made when pure hydrogen was tested versus when a mixture of hydrogen and air was tested.

    (a) Which reaction was more explosive? Why?

    *The mixture of hydrogen and air was more explosive—it produced a loud pop or bang and a recoil effect. In the absence of air mixed with the hydrogen gas, only a soft pop was heard. Hydrogen gas requires oxygen for combustion. The small pop heard when pure hydrogen was ignited was due to hydrogen gas mixing with the surrounding air as it was released from the pipet bulb.*

    (b) Write a balanced chemical equation for the reaction of hydrogen and oxygen.

    $2H_2(g) + O_2(g) \rightarrow 2H_2O(g)$

# Teacher's Notes

Teacher Notes

3. Summarize the physical and chemical properties of hydrogen gas by indicating whether the following statements are True or False:

   (a) Hydrogen gas is colorless. — *True*

   (b) Hydrogen does not diffuse in air. — *False*

   (c) Hydrogen is very soluble in water. — *False*

   (d) Hydrogen has a greater density than air. — *False*

   (e) Hydrogen is flammable. — *True*

   (f) Hydrogen supports combustion. — *False*

   (g) Hydrogen and air will explode when ignited. — *True*

4. The reaction of metals with acids is a general reaction that works with a wide variety of different metals and mineral acids. Write balanced chemical equations for the reactions of:

   (a) Zinc with sulfuric acid.

   $$Zn(s) + H_2SO_4(aq) \rightarrow ZnSO_4(aq) + H_2(g)$$

   (b) Aluminum with hydrochloric acid.

   $$2Al(s) + 6HCl(aq) \rightarrow 2AlCl_3(aq) + 3H_2(g)$$

Preparing and Testing Hydrogen Gas

**Teacher's Notes**

Teacher Notes

## Supplementary Information

### Preparing and Testing Oxygen Gas

Oxygen gas may be generated by the catalytic decomposition of 6% hydrogen peroxide solution. Suitable catalysts include manganese dioxide, manganese, potassium iodide, and yeast.

$$2H_2O_2(aq) \xrightarrow{catalyst} 2H_2O(l) + O_2(g)$$

## Procedure

1. Place about 1 gram of granular manganese dioxide into a small test tube and insert the gas-delivery stopper (see Figure 1).

2. Fill a pipet bulb with water so that the oxygen gas can be collected by the displacement of water.

3. Set up the gas generator as shown in Figure 2. To generate the oxygen gas, remove the gas-delivery stopper and fill the test tube about ⅘ full with 6% hydrogen peroxide solution. Replace the stopper—there should be only a small air space (approximately 1 cm) between the peroxide and the bottom of the stopper. This will reduce the time needed to flush the air out of the gas generator.

4. Place the pipet-bulb full of water on top of the gas delivery stopper to collect the oxygen by water displacement (see Figure 2).

5. Collect a pipet-bulb full of the gas.

6. To test for pure oxygen, bring a pipet-bulb full of the gas to a Bunsen burner, mouth down. Holding the pipet bulb horizontally, place a glowing toothpick into the bulb portion of the pipet bulb. *Note:* A glowing toothpick has no flames, only red embers. Record the observations.

### Test for the Relative Density of Oxygen Compared to Air

7. Collect two pipet-bulbs full of oxygen. Simultaneously hold one pipet bulb right-side up and the other upside down for five minutes. Be sure that the mouths of the bulbs are clear of water.

8. After five minutes, bring the pipet bulbs to a Bunsen burner. Test both pipet bulbs, one at a time, by holding the pipet bulb right-side up and placing a glowing toothpick into the bulb portion of the pipet bulb. Record the observations.

### Test for Mixture of Oxygen and Hydrogen Gases

9. Set up a hydrogen gas generator.

10. Using the same process of water displacement, fill a pipet bulb about ½ full of hydrogen gas, then using the same pipet bulb, fill the remaining half with oxygen gas.

11. To test the mixture, bring a pipet-bulb full of the gases to a Bunsen burner, mouth down. Holding the mouth of the pipet bulb about 2 cm away from the flame of the burner, quickly squeeze the bulb. Record the observations.

Flinn ChemTopic™ Labs — Chemistry of Gases

*Teacher Notes*

# Oxygen, What a Flame
## Microscale Gas Chemistry

### Introduction

Oxygen! We need it to breathe and to survive. Learn how oxygen gas is prepared and observe some interesting properties of the most abundant element on Earth.

### Concepts

- Gas generation
- Oxygen gas
- Combustion
- Oxidation–reduction

### Background

Oxygen gas ($O_2$) is familiar as the second largest component of the Earth's atmosphere (21%). It also occurs as the allotrope $O_3$, called ozone, in the upper atmosphere. Oxygen atoms represent 89% of the mass of a water molecule, making oxygen a key building block of the Earth's water supply (hydrosphere). In addition, much of the Earth's lithosphere (rocks, solid parts of the crust) is composed of silicates, carbonates and oxides that also contain oxygen. Taken together, over 46% of the mass of the lithosphere is oxygen. Because the Earth's surface is bathed in an atmosphere of oxygen, it may seem that oxygen gas is relatively unreactive. In fact, oxygen is the second most reactive of all elements—only fluorine ($F_2$), is more reactive. Oxygen combines directly with all the elements except the halogens, the noble gases, and a few unreactive metals such as gold. Some reactions with oxygen, such as the oxidation of iron, are often slow. On a geological time scale, however, this reaction is fast enough so that there is very little native (metallic) iron present in the Earth's crust.

Oxygen exists as a colorless, odorless, and tasteless gas at room temperature and pressure. It can be condensed to a pale blue liquid by cooling to –183 °C (90 K) at a pressure of one atmosphere. Liquid oxygen, often called LOX, reacts explosively with organic substances and must be handled with great care. At 25 °C oxygen gas dissolves in water to the extent of 31.6 cm³ per liter. It is even more soluble in many non-aqueous solvents.

Photosynthesis accounts for virtually all of the oxygen present in the Earth's atmosphere. Water and carbon dioxide are converted by chloroplasts to oxygen and glucose (Equation 1).

$$6H_2O(l) + 6CO_2(g) \xrightarrow{\text{light energy}} 6O_2(g) + C_6H_{12}O_6(s) \quad \textit{Equation 1}$$

Oxygen supports combustion. This simple phrase has important chemical significance. A combustion reaction is one in which a substance, often an organic hydrocarbon, reacts with oxygen to produce carbon dioxide and water. Combustion reactions are special examples of oxidation–reduction reactions in which so much heat is released that flames are produced. The combustion reaction of methane gas ($CH_4$) in a Bunsen burner flame is represented in Equation 2.

$$CH_4(g) + 2O_2(g) \rightarrow CO_2(g) + 2H_2O(l) + \text{heat} \quad \textit{Equation 2}$$

# Oxygen, What a Flame – Page 2

Even metals are known to "burn" in air. Metals undergo oxidation–reduction reactions with the oxygen in air to produce metal oxides. For example, zinc powder will burn in the flame of a Bunsen burner to form zinc oxide (Equation 3).

$$2Zn(s) + O_2(g) \rightarrow 2ZnO(s) \qquad \text{Equation 3}$$

In this example, zinc metal is oxidized to $Zn^{2+}$ and oxygen gas is reduced to $O^{2-}$ in zinc oxide.

### Experiment Overview

The purpose of this experiment is to collect oxygen gas and test its properties. Oxygen will be generated by the catalytic decomposition of hydrogen peroxide (Equation 4). Potassium iodide will be used as the catalyst.

$$2H_2O_2(aq) \xrightarrow{KI} 2H_2O(l) + O_2(g) \qquad \text{Equation 4}$$

## Pre-Lab Questions

1. Based on the balanced chemical equation for the preparation of oxygen gas, calculate the number of moles of oxygen that can be generated from the reaction of 5 mL of 6% hydrogen peroxide in Part A. Assume that the density of 6% $H_2O_2$ is 1.0 g/mL.

2. Use the ideal gas law equation ($PV = nRT$) to calculate the theoretical volume of oxygen gas that can be generated in Part A. Assume $P = 1.00$ atm, $T = 298$ K, and $R = 0.0821$ L·atm/mol·K.

## Materials

| | |
|---|---|
| "Blue bottle" solution, 30 mL | Matches |
| Hydrogen peroxide solution, $H_2O_2$, 6%, 50 mL | Pinchcock clamp (for tubing) |
| Limewater, $Ca(OH)_2$, saturated solution, 15 mL | Ring stand with clamp |
| Potassium iodide powder, KI, 0.5 g | Silicone grease |
| Steel wool, Fe, small wad | Spatula |
| Tap water | Stopper, one-hole |
| Beakers, 100-mL, 2 | Syringe, 60-mL |
| Bunsen burner | Syringe tip cap, latex |
| Candle, small | Test tube, Pyrex®, extra large |
| Forceps | Vial cap, plastic |
| Latex tubing | Wood splint |

## Safety Precautions

*Gases in the syringe may be under pressure and could spray liquid chemicals. Follow the instructions and use only the quantities suggested. Hydrogen peroxide solution is an oxidizer and a skin and eye irritant. The "blue bottle" solution contains potassium hydroxide and is slightly corrosive to skin and eyes. Avoid contact of all chemicals with skin and eyes. Wear chemical splash goggles and chemical-resistant gloves and apron. Wash hands thoroughly with soap and water before leaving the laboratory.*

---

**Teacher Notes**

*The theoretical volume of oxygen that can be produced in Part A is almost double the 60-mL volume of the syringe. The reaction, however, is quite slow and does not pose a safety hazard if students watch the syringe and stop the reaction when they have collected the desired amount of oxygen gas.*

Teacher Notes

**Procedure**

*Part A. Preparation of Oxygen Gas*

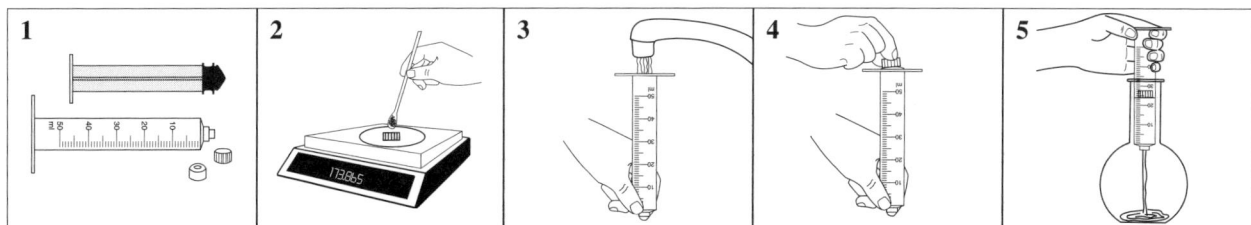

1. Inspect the syringe before use—make sure that the plunger moves freely in the syringe, and that both the plunger seal and syringe are free from cracks. If necessary, lubricate the rubber seal with a thin film of silicone grease to allow the plunger to move freely. (Lubricate only the edge that makes contact with the inner barrel wall.)

2. Measure out 0.10 g of potassium iodide and place it into a plastic vial cap. Avoid getting any chemical on the sides of the vial cap.

3. Remove the plunger from the syringe barrel. Hold your finger over the tip of the syringe. Fill syringe completely with tap water. The water should be even with the top of the syringe.

4. Carefully place the vial cap containing the solid reagent face up on the surface of the water so that the cap floats.

5. Remove your finger from the syringe opening and allow the water to flow out of the syringe into a waste flask or a beaker. As the water level decreases, the vial cap will be lowered to the bottom of the syringe. The cap should come to rest upright on the bottom of the syringe with all of the reagent still in the cap. *Note:* If the vial cap tips over and the solid spills out, clean out the syringe and start over.

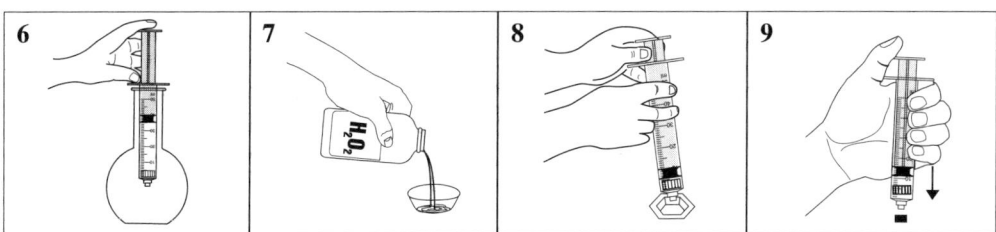

6. Carefully replace the plunger while maintaining the syringe in a vertical position. Gently push the plunger in as far as it will go—this will anchor the vial cap into the depression at the base of the syringe. *Note:* There is a point just after the plunger's rubber diaphragm enters the barrel where there will be resistance. Gently but firmly push the plunger past this point.

7. Pour about 10 mL of 6% hydrogen peroxide solution into a weighing dish or small beaker.

8. Draw about 5 mL of the hydrogen peroxide solution into the syringe. Be careful that the vial cap does not tip over since it will cause the reaction to begin prematurely.

9. Secure the latex syringe cap on the tip of the syringe by setting the syringe cap on the counter and quickly pushing the syringe into the cap.

*The preparation of oxygen gas is a relatively slow reaction. Shaking the syringe and gently pulling on the plunger will speed the process. Caution students not to leave the syringe unattended during this time.*

**Oxygen, What a Flame** – Page 4

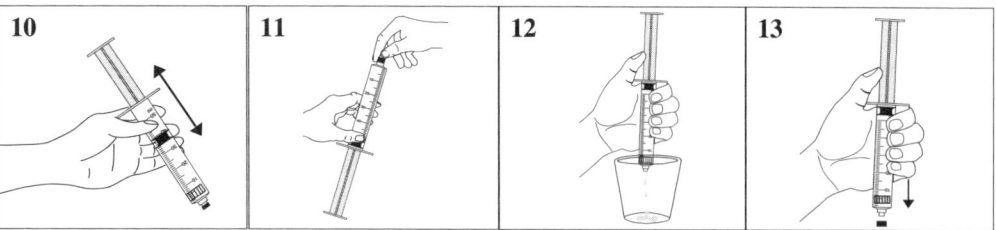

10. Read Step 11 now to understand how to stop the reaction. Do this before going on. Shake the syringe vigorously to mix the reagents and initiate the reaction. The plunger will slowly move outward as it is displaced by the gas. *Caution:* Do not leave the syringe unattended while the reaction takes place.

11. The next three steps (11, 12, and 13) should be performed quickly to minimize loss of oxygen gas. When the reaction is completed or the volume of gas is about 50–60 mL, tip the syringe up to stop the reaction, and then remove the syringe cap. If the reaction occurs too rapidly, or generates more than 50–60 mL of gas, immediately stop gas collection by using the *tilt, twist,* and *release* procedure. *Tilt* the syringe so the tip is pointing upward but away from anyone. *Twist* off the syringe cap with a slight twist and *release* the pressure.

12. Hold the syringe with the tip pointing downward. Discharge the liquid reagents into the sink or a beaker. Use caution during this step so that none of the gas is discharged.

13. Secure the latex syringe cap back on the tip of the syringe.

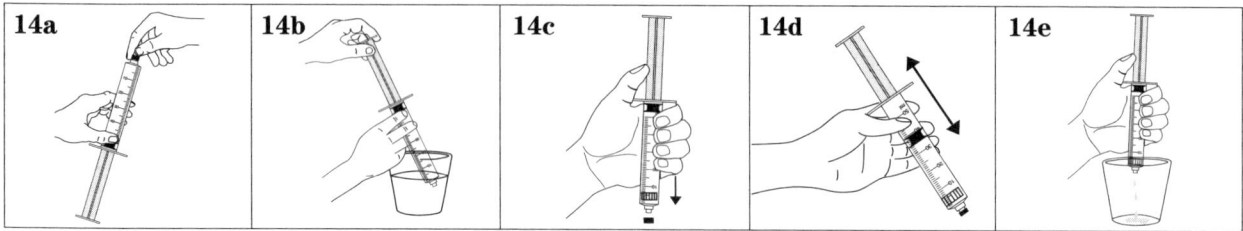

14. After preparing the oxygen gas, wash the inside of the syringe in order to remove excess reactants. Follow the steps below and repeat if necesssary.

    (a) Remove the syringe cap with the tip of the syringe pointing up.

    (b) Draw a few mL of water into the syringe.

    (c) Recap the syringe.

    (d) Shake the syringe to wash the inside surfaces.

    (e) Remove the syringe cap and discharge the water only into the sink or a beaker. *Note:* Do not depress the plunger fully or the gas will be lost. Recap the syringe to continue.

Teacher Notes

*Washing the gas inside the syringe removes excess reactants and will not affect the properties of the desired gas. Oxygen gas generated in Part A can be stored in the sealed syringe for several days.*

*Page 5 –* **Oxygen, What a Flame**

Teacher Notes

### Part B. Oxygen and Combustion

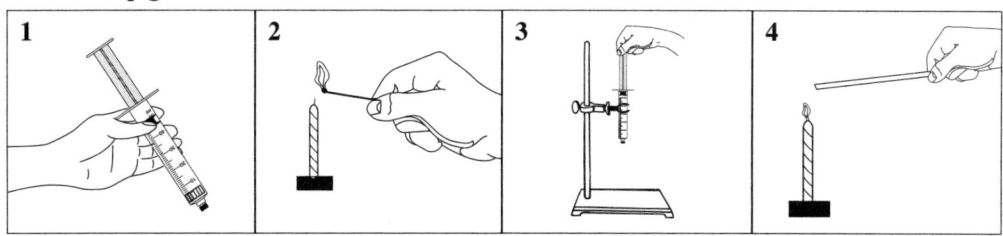

1. Collect about 60 mL of oxygen gas from Part A.

2. Place a candle in a one-hole stopper to stand it up. Light the candle and set it aside.

3. Clamp the syringe firmly in a vertical position with the plunger end up and the sealed tip pointing downward. Carefully remove the plunger from the syringe.

4. Use the candle to light the wood splint.

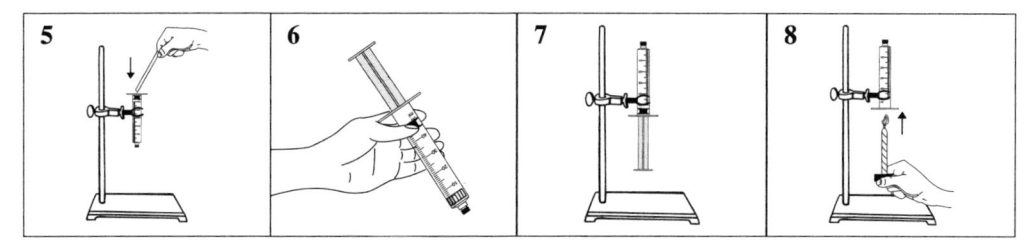

5. Blow the flaming splint out. Immediately plunge the glowing splint into the $O_2$-filled syringe. Lift the splint slightly out and again plunge the splint into the syringe. Record your observations in the data table.

6. Repeat Part A to collect another syringeful (about 60 mL) of oxygen gas.

7. Clamp the syringe in a vertical position. This time the plunger end should be in the down position with the sealed tip pointing upward.

8. Remove the plunger from the syringe. Immediately raise the lit candle into the $O_2$-filled syringe. Wait for the flame to extinguish before removing the candle. Record your observations in the data table.

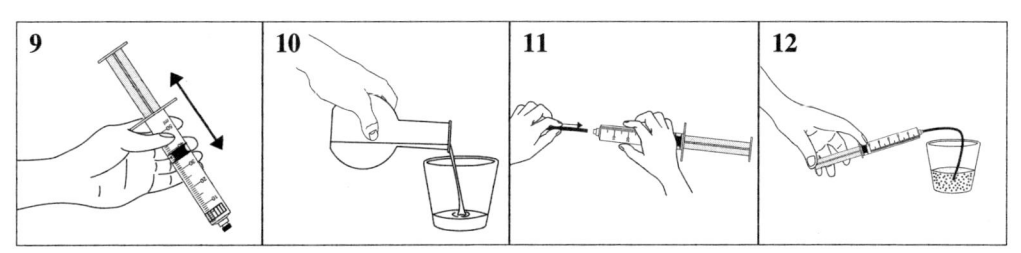

9. Re-install the plunger into the syringe barrel just until the rubber seal is at the 60-mL mark. *Note:* Do not refill the syringe with oxygen. This is a test to determine what gas is currently in the syringe.

10. Fill a small beaker with 15 mL of fresh limewater.

11. Remove the syringe cap and quickly attach a piece of latex tubing to the syringe.

12. Bubble all of the gas from the syringe through the limewater solution. Record your observations in the data table.

Oxygen, What a Flame

**Oxygen, What a Flame** – Page 6

### Part C. Steel Wool and Oxygen

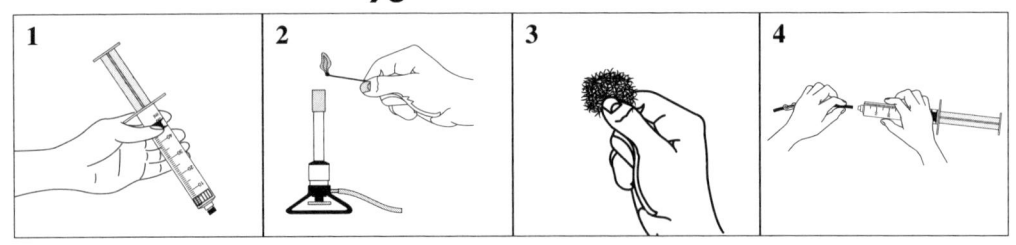

1. Repeat Part A to collect a third syringeful (about 60 mL) of oxygen gas.

2. Light a Bunsen burner and set aside for use in Step 6.

3. Wearing gloves, gently pull apart the steel wool fibers to make a small ball of steel wool.

4. Remove the cap from the syringe of oxygen gas and attach a piece of latex tubing closed off with a clamp.

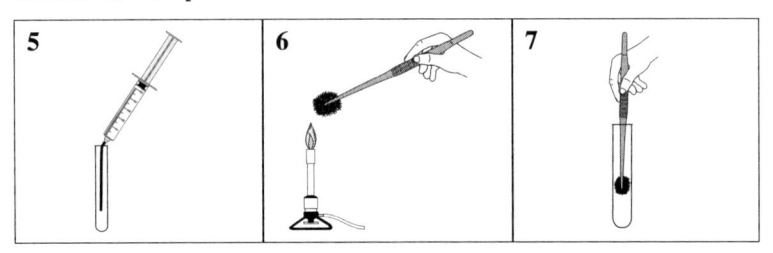

5. Release the tubing clamp and place the latex tubing into the bottom of an extra large Pyrex® test tube. Allow the oxygen gas to flow into the bottom of the test tube.

6. Hold the steel wool ball with forceps and ignite a small surface area with the burner.

7. Immediately plunge the glowing steel wool ball into the test tube filled with oxygen. Record your observations in the data table.

### Part D. The "Blue-Bottle" Reaction in a Syringe

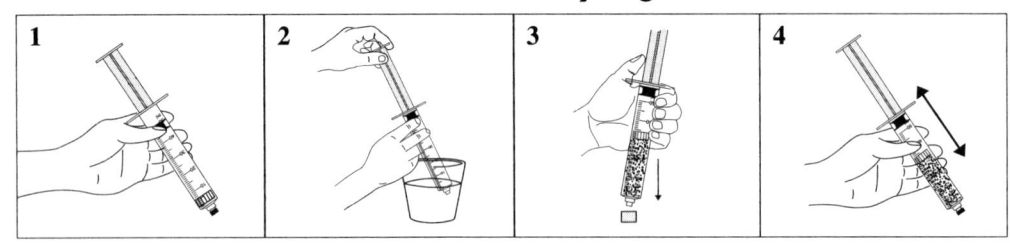

1. Repeat Part A and collect about 40 mL of oxygen gas in the syringe.

2. Pour 30 mL of "blue bottle" solution into a 100-mL beaker. Remove the latex cap from the syringe and draw 25 mL of the "blue bottle" solution into the syringe.

3. Securely replace the syringe cap on the tip of the syringe.

4. Shake the syringe *once* and observe the color of the solution. Holding the syringe still, observe what happens to the color of the solution over the next several minutes.

5. Shake the syringe again and observe any color change. Repeat as needed to deduce the purpose of the shaking. Record your observations in the data table.

---

Teacher Notes

*In Part C, caution students to ignite only a small surface portion of the steel wool in the Bunsen burner flame. Students should work in pairs—let one student release the oxygen gas into the test tube in step 5, while the other student simultaneously heats the steel wool in step 6 and plunges it into the test tube. The steel wool ball will burst into flame in the bottom of the test tube. Check to make sure that the test tube is made of heat-resistant borosilicate glass (Pryex®).*

*Page 7 – **Oxygen, What a Flame***

Teacher Notes

Name: _____

Class/Lab Period: _____

# Oxygen, What a Flame

**Data Table**

|        | Reactants | Observations |
|--------|-----------|--------------|
| Part A |           |              |
| Part B |           |              |
| Part C |           |              |
| Part D |           |              |

# Oxygen, What a Flame – Page 8

**Post-Lab Questions** *(Use a separate sheet of paper to answer the following questions.)*

1. What chemical property of oxygen was illustrated in Part B? What type of reaction occurred?

2. What happened to the candle flame in Part B? Explain your observations.

3. What gases replaced the oxygen in the syringe in Part B? How do you know?

4. Write the chemical equation for the reaction between the gas produced in Part B and limewater.

5. Does the steel wool burn faster in the air or in pure oxygen? Explain.

6. (a) Predict what would happen if you were to use coarse steel wool instead of fine steel wool in Part C. (b) Predict what would happen if you were to use iron powder instead of steel wool.

7. Write the balanced equation for the reaction in Part C. Assume that the main product contains iron(III).

8. What was the purpose of shaking the syringe containing the oxygen and the "blue bottle" solution in Part D?

9. Did oxygen gas cause the solution to become blue or colorless? What type of reaction occurred?

Teacher Notes

# Teacher's Notes
## Oxygen, What a Flame

### Master Materials List

| | |
|---|---|
| Dextrose solution, 0.4 M, 250 mL* | Forceps, 15 |
| Hydrogen peroxide solution, $H_2O_2$, 6%, 1 L† | Gas-collecting supplies§ |
| Limewater, $Ca(OH)_2$, saturated solution, 250 mL† | Gas generating vial caps, plastic, 15 |
| Methylene blue solution, 3 mL* | Latex tubing, 6″, 15 pieces |
| Potassium hydroxide solution, KOH, 1 M, 250 mL* | Syringes, 60-mL, 15 |
| Potassium iodide, KI, 10 g | Syringe tip caps, latex, 15 |
| Steel wool, Fe, 1 pad | Matches, 15 |
| Tap water | Ring stands with clamps, 15 |
| Balances, centigram (0.01-g precision) | Silicone grease, 1 packet |
| Beakers, 100-mL, 30 | Spatulas, 15 |
| Bunsen burners, 15 | Stoppers, one-hole, 15 |
| Candles, small, pkg 24 | Test tubes, 25 × 200 mm, Pyrex®, 15 |
| Clamps, pinchcock-type, 15 | Wood splints, 30 |

*These solutions are needed to prepare the "blue-bottle" solution for student use. See the *Preparation of Solutions* section.

†We recommend the purchase of ready-made hydrogen peroxide (Flinn Catalog No. H0028) and limewater (Flinn Catalog No. L0021) solutions.

§All of the materials listed under the gas-collecting supplies are provided in the "Classroom Equipment Kit" for microscale gas chemistry (Flinn Catalog No. AP5951).

### Preparation of Solutions

*"Blue Bottle" Solution:* Prepare the "blue bottle" solution fresh on the day of the lab. In a 500-mL flask, mix together 250 mL of the dextrose solution with 250 mL of the potassium hydroxide solution. Add 15–20 drops of the methylene blue indicator solution. Label the flask as the "blue-bottle" solution. *Note:* If less "blue bottle" solution is needed for the class, use proportionally less of each chemical. Once mixed, the solution is not stable for more than one day.

### Safety Precautions

*Gases in the syringe may be under pressure and could spray liquid chemicals. Follow the instructions and use only the quantities suggested. Hydrogen peroxide solution is an oxidizer and a skin and eye irritant. The "blue-bottle" solution contains potassium hydroxide and is slightly corrosive to skin and eyes. Avoid contact of all chemicals with skin and eyes. Wear chemical splash goggles and chemical-resistant gloves and apron. Remind students to wash their hands thoroughly with soap and water before leaving the laboratory. Please consult current Material Safety Data Sheets for additional safety, handling, and disposal information.*

# Teacher's Notes

## Disposal

Please consult your current *Flinn Scientific Catalog/Reference Manual* for general guidelines and specific procedures governing the disposal of laboratory waste. Excess oxygen can be released into the air. Excess reagents can be rinsed down the drain with plenty of water according to Flinn Suggested Disposal Method #26b.

## Lab Hints

- The oxygen gas that is generated can be stored in the sealed syringe for extended periods of time.

- Demonstrate the procedure for washing oxygen. Washing the gas removes excess reagents from the syringe, which could affect any of the experiments involving oxygen. Supply a waste beaker at each lab table for the wastewater from the washings.

- After completing Part A (generating oxygen gas), students may wonder why the solution in the syringe is yellow. This color is due to iodine, $I_2$, which is formed as a byproduct of the reaction. The iodide ion is oxidized to iodine by hydrogen peroxide. The yellow color will eventually disappear when the catalyst is regenerated.

- The purpose of Part B is to show that oxygen is needed for combustion reactions and that one of the major products of combustion is carbon dioxide. The balanced equation for the combustion reaction of one of the volatile components of wax is as follows:
$C_{25}H_{52}(g) + 38O_2(g) \rightarrow 25CO_2(g) + 26H_2O(g)$.

- The limewater provided to students for Part B should be clear. If the stock limewater is agitated and the solution turns cloudy, allow the solution to settle. Decant the solution and use only the clear liquid for the test. Students should obtain the limewater just prior to performing Part B. If allowed to sit out on the lab bench, the limewater will gradually turn cloudy from the carbon dioxide in the air.

- Check to make sure that the test tubes provided for Part C are made of heat-resistant borosilicate (e.g., Pyrex®) glass.

- The "blue bottle" experiment in Part D is an oxidation–reduction reaction. The conversion of the colorless, reduced form of methylene blue to the blue, oxidized form occurs when there is oxygen in the solution:

$$\text{Methylene blue} + O_2(aq) \rightarrow \text{Methylene blue} + H_2O(l)$$
$$\text{Colorless} \qquad\qquad\qquad\qquad \text{Blue}$$

Upon shaking, which adds oxygen to the solution, the solution turns from colorless to blue as methylene blue is oxidized and oxygen gas is reduced. Shaking the syringe causes more $O_2(g)$ to dissolve in the water. Upon standing undisturbed, dextrose reduces the blue methylene blue back to the colorless form:

$$\text{Methylene blue} + \text{Dextrose} \rightarrow \text{Methylene blue} + \text{Dextrose oxidation products}$$
$$\text{Blue} \qquad\qquad\qquad\qquad \text{Colorless}$$

The oxidation–reduction process can be repeated many times.

**Teacher's Notes**

Teacher Notes

**Teaching Tips**

- For additional oxidation–reduction demonstrations similar to the "blue-bottle" reaction, see the following chemical demonstration kits available from Flinn Scientific: "Feeling Blue" (Catalog No. AP8653), "Stop-'N-Go Light" (Catalog No. AP2083), and "Vanishing Valentine" (Catalog No. AP5929).

- See the following reference for additional information and experiments utilizing microscale "gases in a syringe." Mattson, Bruce; Anderson, Michael; and Schwennsen, Cece *Chemistry of Gases: A Microscale Approach,* Flinn Scientific: Batavia, IL (2002).

**Answers to Pre-Lab Questions** *(Student answers will vary.)*

1. Based on the balanced chemical equation for the preparation of oxygen gas, calculate the number of moles of oxygen that can be generated from the reaction of 5 mL of 6% hydrogen peroxide in Part A. Assume that the density of 6% $H_2O_2$ is 1.0 g/mL.

$$2H_2O_2(aq) \xrightarrow{KI} 2H_2O(l) + O_2(g)$$

$$5\ mL \times \frac{1.0\ g}{mL} = 5\ g \times .06 = 0.30\ g\ H_2O_2$$

$$0.30\ g\ H_2O_2 \times \frac{1\ mol}{34.02\ g} = 0.0088\ moles\ of\ H_2O_2$$

$$0.0088\ moles\ H_2O_2 \times \frac{1\ mole\ O_2}{2\ moles\ H_2O_2} = 0.0044\ moles\ of\ O_2$$

2. Use the ideal gas law equation ($PV = nRT$) to calculate the theoretical volume of oxygen gas that can be generated in Part A. Assume $P$ = 1.00 atm, $T$ = 298 K, and $R$ = 0.0821 L·atm/mol·K.

$$V = nRT/P = \frac{(0.0044\ mol)(0.0821\ L\cdot atm/mol\cdot K)(298\ K)}{1.00\ atm}$$

$V$ = 0.11 L (110 mL) *of oxygen gas is expected.*

# Teacher's Notes

## Sample Data

*Student data will vary.*

### Data Table

|  | **Reactants** | **Observations** |
|---|---|---|
| **Part A** | KI(s) and $H_2O_2$(l) | Solution bubbled and syringe plunger moved out slowly as gas was produced. Solution turned pale yellow. |
| **Part B** | Candle<br>$O_2$(g)<br>Limewater | Step 5: Glowing splint re-ignited when placed in oxygen.<br><br>Step 8: Candle burned very brightly for a few seconds, but then extinguished when the oxygen was used up.<br><br>Step 12: Limewater turned cloudy. |
| **Part C** | Bunsen burner flame<br>Steel wool<br>$O_2$(g) | Glowing steel wool burst into flame when it was inserted into the test tube filled with pure oxygen gas. |
| **Part D** | "Blue-bottle" solution<br>$O_2$(g) | Solution turned blue when the syringe containing oxygen gas was shaken.<br><br>Solution turned colorless when allowed to sit undisturbed. The process could be repeated numerous times. |

Teacher Notes

# Teacher's Notes

**Answers to Post-Lab Questions** *(Student answers will vary.)*

1. What chemical property of oxygen was illustrated in Part B? What type of reaction occurred?

    *Chemical property: Oxygen is required for combustion to occur.*

    *Sample combustion reaction between a hydrocarbon component of wax and oxygen:*

    $C_{25}H_{52}(g) + 38O_2(g) \rightarrow 25CO_2(g) + 26H_2O(g)$

2. What happened to the candle flame in Part B? Explain your observations.

    *At first the flame burned brightly in pure oxygen. The flame then went out, however, after all the oxygen in the syringe had reacted.*

3. What gases replaced the oxygen in the syringe in Part B? How do you know?

    *The products of combustion are carbon dioxide and water, which replaced the oxygen in the syringe. Carbon dioxide gas in the syringe gave a characteristic positive test with limewater.*

4. Write the reaction between the gas produced in Part B and limewater.

    $CO_2(g) + Ca(OH)_2(aq) \rightarrow CaCO_3(s) + H_2O(l)$

5. Does the steel wool burn faster in the air or in pure oxygen? Explain.

    *In the experiment, oxygen reacted with the iron in the steel wool. The reaction was much faster in pure oxygen than in air. Reaction rates depend on the concentration of the reactants—increasing the concentration of oxygen gas made the reaction go faster.*

6. (a) Predict what would happen if you were to use coarse steel wool instead of fine steel wool in Part C. (b) Predict what would happen if you were to use iron powder instead of steel wool.

    *Reaction rates also depend on the particle size of the reactants. The reaction will go faster using smaller-sized iron particles. The coarse steel wool has much larger iron fibers and would react very slowly while the powdered iron has the smallest particles and would react very fast (explosively).*

7. Write the balanced equation for the reaction in Part C. Assume that the main product contains iron(III).

    *The reactants are iron and oxygen. The product is iron(III) oxide, $Fe_2O_3$.*

    $4Fe(s) + 3O_2(g) \rightarrow 2Fe_2O_3(s)$

8. What was the purpose of shaking the syringe containing the oxygen and the "blue bottle" solution in Part D?

    *Shaking the syringe caused more of the oxygen gas to dissolve in the aqueous phase. The concentration of oxygen increased.*

# Teacher's Notes

9. Did oxygen gas cause the solution to become blue or colorless? What type of reaction occurred?

   *Oxygen caused the solution to turn blue. This is an oxidation–reduction reaction between the dissolved oxygen and methylene blue, a redox indicator.* **Note to teachers:** *Use your discretion in deciding how much of the chemistry to explain to students before they observe the "blue bottle" reaction in the syringe. Students will be motivated to study the process more carefully if they do not know the "right" answer before they start.*

## Supplementary Information

The microscale syringe method provides a safe way for students to study the properties of a variety of gases in the high school laboratory. Each gas takes no more than five minutes to generate and is then immediately available for testing.

Gas Generation Equipment
- Plastic syringe, 60-mL, with luer lock fitting
- Luer lock syringe cap
- Plastic vial cap that fits within the barrel of the syringe (made of inert material)
- Weighing dish or boat
- Beaker or cup, 250-mL
- Latex tubing (⅛-inch ID), 15-cm length
- Silicone grease

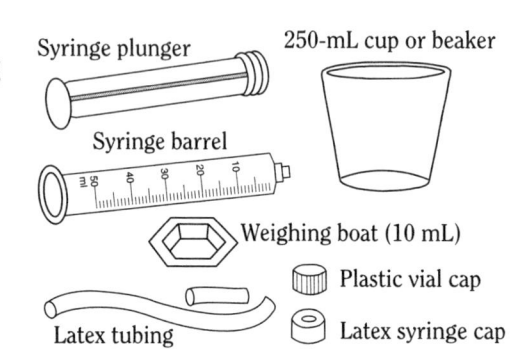

All activities are scaled to use a plastic 60-mL syringe with a luer lock fitting. New syringes come packaged with a plastic syringe cover. The plastic syringe cover will not function as a syringe cap and should be discarded. New syringes may be stiff—"break" in the syringe by moving the plunger up and down in the barrel several times to loosen the apparatus and allow for unrestricted motion. The latex syringe cap is reusable but does stretch out over time. If the cap does not fit tightly, it needs to be replaced.

The following table summarizes the reagents and amounts needed to prepare common gases.

| Gas | Solid Reagent | Amount | Liquid Reagent | Amount |
|---|---|---|---|---|
| $CO_2$ | $NaHCO_3$ | 0.22 g | 1 M HCl | 5 mL |
| $H_2$ | Mg powder | 0.07 g | 1 M HCl | 5 mL |
| $O_2$ | KI (catalyst) | 0.10 g | 6% $H_2O_2$ | 5 mL |
| $N_2$ | $HSO_3NH_2$ | 0.20 g | 0.5 M $NaNO_2$ | 5 mL |
| $C_2H_2$ | $CaC_2$ | 0.20 g | $H_2O$ | 5 mL |

*Teacher Notes*

# Carbon Dioxide, What a Gas
## Microscale Gas Chemistry

### Introduction

Prepare carbon dioxide gas, perform the classic limewater test for the detection of carbon dioxide, and observe its acidic nature. Watch the gas undergo a chemical reaction and determine if carbon dioxide supports combustion of a candle flame.

### Concepts

- Preparation of gases
- Combustion
- Carbon dioxide gas
- Acid–base reactions

### Background

Carbon dioxide, a colorless gas, is present in our atmosphere at very low levels. Although it is essentially odorless as well, carbon dioxide causes a sharp sensation when inhaled in concentrated doses. This may be noticed if the fizzy bubbles from a freshly poured carbonated beverage are inhaled.

Carbon dioxide was discovered over 250 years ago by an Englishman, Joseph Black, who collected and studied the gas produced when chalk (calcium carbonate, $CaCO_3$) was heated (Equation 1). Black found that the chalk lost mass when it was heated, and that this loss corresponded to the escape of a gas. He called the gas that was produced "fixed air," because it had different properties than ordinary air.

$$CaCO_3(s) \rightarrow CaO(s) + CO_2(g) \qquad \textit{Equation 1}$$

Joseph Black also determined that the same gas was produced by the action of acids on carbonates, from fermenting vegetables, and when coal was burned. The reaction of calcium carbonate with hydrochloric acid, for example, produces carbon dioxide gas, as shown in Equation 2.

$$CaCO_3(s) + 2HCl(aq) \rightarrow CaCl_2(aq) + H_2O(l) + CO_2(g) \qquad \textit{Equation 2}$$

In popular lectures on the nature of "fixed air," Black further demonstrated that carbon dioxide was present in exhaled breath and that it was a byproduct of respiration, both in plants and animals. In 1771 Joseph Priestley extended this work and determined that plants could "purify" air by consuming carbon dioxide gas and producing a new gas, oxygen. We now know that this is due to photosynthesis (Equation 3). Black's experiments with carbon dioxide gas are noteworthy for several reasons, not the least of which is that carbon dioxide gas was the first pure gas to be isolated and studied.

$$6CO_2(g) + 6H_2O(l) \rightarrow C_6H_{12}O_6(aq) + 6O_2(g) \qquad \textit{Equation 3}$$

Carbon dioxide is one of the normal products of combustion. For example, when carbon burns in air, it produces carbon dioxide and heat via the following exothermic reaction (Equation 4):

$$C(s) + O_2(g) \rightarrow CO_2(g) + 394 \text{ kJ/mole} \qquad \textit{Equation 4}$$

Carbon Dioxide, What a Gas

# Carbon Dioxide, What a Gas – Page 2

Other carbon-containing fuels such as gasoline and natural gas produce carbon dioxide and water upon combustion. Natural gas is primarily methane, $CH_4(g)$. The chemical equation for the combustion of methane is shown in Equation 5.

$$CH_4(g) + 2O_2(g) \rightarrow CO_2(g) + 2H_2O(g) + 803 \text{ kJ/mole} \qquad \textit{Equation 5}$$

It is known that carbon dioxide gas present in the upper atmosphere traps heat and thus acts like a global blanket. The sun warms the surface of the Earth and the heat normally radiates back out into space. Because low levels of $CO_2(g)$ are naturally present in the Earth's atmosphere, a certain amount of this blanket effect is normal. However, the widespread combustion of fossil fuels in our modern world has produced vast quantities of carbon dioxide gas, thus thickening the blanket. Much of the heat energy ends up trapped in our atmosphere. In the past century, the amount of carbon dioxide in our atmosphere has increased to the point where scientists are concerned that our planet is slowly warming up. This phenomenon is called the greenhouse effect and is associated with global warming.

Carbon dioxide has many important commercial uses. It is used as a refrigerant, in the soft drink industry, as a chemical reagent to make other compounds, and in fire extinguishers. The major industrial use of carbon dioxide—accounting for more than 50% of the $CO_2$ produced— is as a refrigerant. Dry ice, $CO_2(s)$, was first commercially introduced as a refrigerant in 1924. Dry ice sublimes to a gas at –78.5 °C at standard pressure. By the 1960s, dry ice had been replaced by liquid carbon dioxide (commonly called liquid carbonic) as the most common $CO_2$ refrigerant. Carbon dioxide has a melting point of –56.6 °C at 5.2 atmospheres. Liquid $CO_2$ is used to freeze materials such as hamburger meat and metals. It is also used to rapidly cool loaded trucks and rail cars. About 25% of all $CO_2$ produced is used in the soft drink industry. Carbon dioxide is also widely used as a replacement for the propellant in aerosol cans that were formerly charged with chlorofluorocarbons (CFCs).

The solubility of carbon dioxide gas in water is 3.48 g per liter at 0 °C and 1.45 g per liter at 25 °C. Dissolved carbon dioxide is represented as $CO_2(aq)$ (Equation 6).

$$CO_2(g) \rightleftharpoons CO_2(aq) \qquad \textit{Equation 6}$$

Solutions of $CO_2(aq)$ last longer if they are kept cool. As the solution of $CO_2(aq)$ is warmed, $CO_2(g)$ is released as bubbles. This is noticeable when a carbonated beverage is warmed.

A very small portion of dissolved carbon dioxide reacts with water to produce carbonic acid, $H_2CO_3$, which dissociates to hydrogen ($H^+$) and bicarbonate ($HCO_3^-$) ions (Equation 7).

$$CO_2(aq) + H_2O(l) \rightleftharpoons H_2CO_3(aq) \rightleftharpoons H^+(aq) + HCO_3^-(aq) \qquad \textit{Equation 7}$$

For this reason, dissolved carbon dioxide is described as being "weakly acidic." The acid–base equilibrium shown in Equation 7 functions as the buffer system in blood.

The bicarbonate ion, which is also called hydrogen carbonate, and the carbonate ion ($CO_3^{2-}$), have a vast and useful chemistry. Both ions are made when carbon dioxide reacts with an alkaline (basic) solution such as sodium hydroxide.

$$CO_2(aq) + NaOH(aq) \rightarrow NaHCO_3(aq) \qquad \textit{Equation 8}$$

$$CO_2(aq) + 2NaOH(aq) \rightarrow Na_2CO_3(aq) + H_2O(l) \qquad \textit{Equation 9}$$

Teacher Notes

Teacher Notes

### Experiment Overview

The purpose of this experiment is to prepare carbon dioxide gas and study its properties. Carbon dioxide will be generated by the reaction of solid sodium bicarbonate with hydrochloric acid.

### Pre-Lab Questions

1. Write the balanced chemical equation for the gas-generating reaction in Part A.

2. When 0.22 g of $NaHCO_3$ and 5.0 mL of 1.0 M HCl are used in Part A, which reactant is the limiting reactant? Show all work.

3. What type of reaction occurs in the syringe in Part A—oxidation–reduction, acid–base, or precipitation?

### Materials

| | |
|---|---|
| Ammonia, $NH_3(g)$ from 6 M $NH_4OH$ solution | Latex tubing |
| Hydrochloric acid solution, HCl, 1 M, 30 mL | Matches |
| Limewater, $Ca(OH)_2$, saturated solution, 10–15 mL | Ring stand with clamp |
| Sodium bicarbonate, $NaHCO_3$, 0.66 g | Silicone grease |
| Sodium hydroxide solution, NaOH, 6 M, 10 mL | Spatula |
| Universal indicator solution, 1 mL | Stirring rod, glass |
| Universal indicator color card (1 for the class) | Syringe, 60-mL |
| Balance | Syringe tip cap, latex |
| Beakers, 100-mL, 2 | Tap water |
| Beral-type pipet | Tape |
| Candle, small | Vial cap, plastic |

### Safety Precautions

*Gases in the syringe may be under pressure and could spray liquid chemicals. Follow the instructions and use only the quantities suggested. Ammonium hydroxide and hydrochloric acid solutions are toxic by inhalation and ingestion, and are corrosive to all body tissues. Notify the teacher and clean up all spills immediately. Ammonia fumes can burn nasal membranes; always handle ammonia solutions in an operating fume hood. Sodium hydroxide is a corrosive liquid and is especially dangerous to skin and eyes. Avoid contact of all chemicals with skin and eyes. Wear chemical splash goggles and chemical-resistant gloves and apron. Wash hands thoroughly with soap and water before leaving the laboratory.*

# Carbon Dioxide, What a Gas – Page 4

**Procedure**

Teacher Notes

### Part A. Preparation of Carbon Dioxide Gas

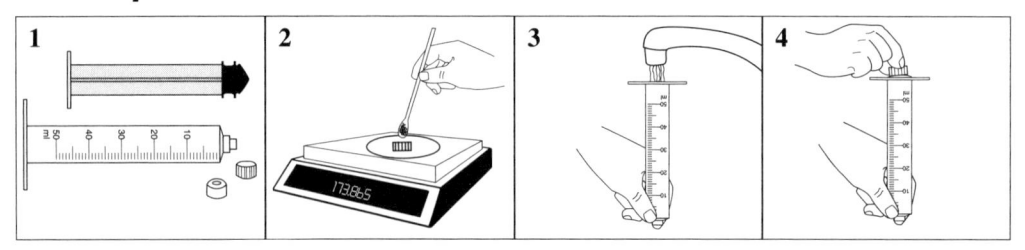

1. Inspect the syringe before use—make sure that the plunger moves freely in the syringe, and that both the plunger seal and syringe are free from cracks. If necessary, lubricate the rubber seal with a thin film of silicone grease to allow the plunger to move freely. (Lubricate only the edge that makes contact with the inner barrel wall.)

2. Measure out 0.22 g of sodium bicarbonate and place it into a plastic vial cap. Avoid getting any chemical on the sides of the vial cap.

3. Remove the plunger from the syringe barrel. Hold your finger over the tip of the syringe. Fill syringe completely with tap water. The water should be even with the top of the syringe.

4. Carefully place the vial cap containing the solid reagent face up on the surface of the water so that the cap floats.

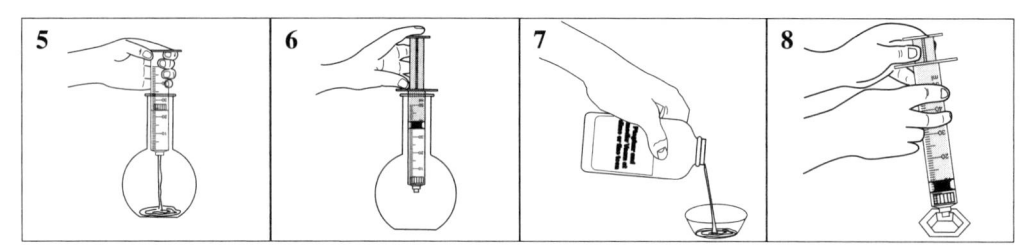

5. Remove your finger from the syringe opening and allow the water to flow out of the syringe into a waste flask or a beaker. As the water level decreases, the vial cap will be lowered to the bottom of the syringe. The cap should come to rest upright on the bottom of the syringe with all of the reagent still in the cap. *Note:* If the vial cap tips over and the solid spills out, clean out the syringe and start over.

6. Carefully replace the plunger while maintaining the syringe in a vertical position. Gently push the plunger in as far as it will go. It will anchor the vial cap into the depression at the base of the syringe. *Note:* There is a point just after the plunger's rubber diaphragm enters the barrel where there will be resistance. Gently, but firmly, push the plunger past this point.

7. Pour about 10 mL of 1 M hydrochloric acid into a small beaker.

8. Draw about 5 mL of 1 M hydrochloric acid solution into the syringe. Be careful that the vial cap does not tip over since it will cause the reaction to begin prematurely.

*Carbon dioxide gas generated in Part A can be stored in the sealed syringe for several days.*

*Page 5 –* **Carbon Dioxide, What a Gas**

Teacher Notes

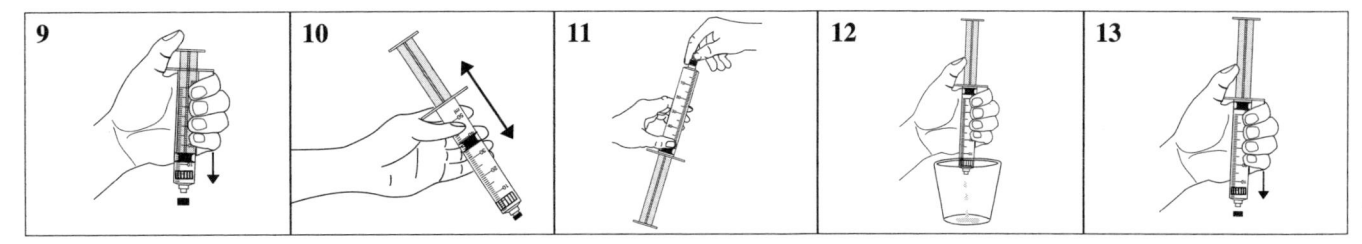

9. Secure the latex syringe cap on the tip of the syringe by setting the syringe cap on the counter and quickly pushing the syringe into the cap.

10. Read Step 11 now to understand how to stop the reaction. Do this before going on. Shake the syringe vigorously to mix the reagents and initiate the reaction. The plunger will slowly move outward as it is displaced by the gas. *Caution:* Do not leave the syringe unattended while the reaction takes place.

11. The next three steps (11, 12, and 13) should be performed quickly to minimize loss of carbon dioxide gas. When the reaction is completed or the volume of gas is about 50–60 mL, tip the syringe up to stop the reaction, and then remove the syringe cap. If the reaction occurs too rapidly, or generates more than 50–60 mL of gas, stop gas collection by using the *tilt, twist,* and *release* procedure. *Tilt* the syringe so the tip is pointing upward but away from anyone. *Twist* off the syringe cap with a slight twist and *release* the pressure.

12. Hold the syringe with the tip pointing downward. Discharge the liquid reagents into the sink or a beaker. Use caution during this step so that none of the gas is discharged.

13. Secure the latex syringe cap back on the tip of the syringe.

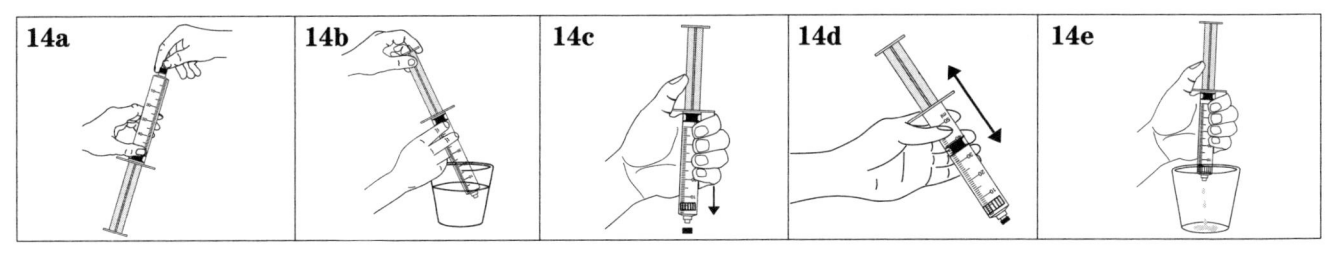

14. Wash the inside of the syringe in order to remove excess reagents. Follow the steps below and repeat if necesssary.

    (a) Remove the syringe cap with the tip of the syringe pointing up.

    (b) Draw a few mL of water into the syringe.

    (c) Recap the syringe.

    (d) Shake the syringe to wash the inside surfaces.

    (e) Remove the syringe cap and discharge the water only into the sink or a beaker.
    *Note:* Do not depress the plunger fully or the gas will be lost. Recap the syringe to continue.

# Carbon Dioxide, What a Gas – Page 6

### Part B. Classic Test for Carbon Dioxide

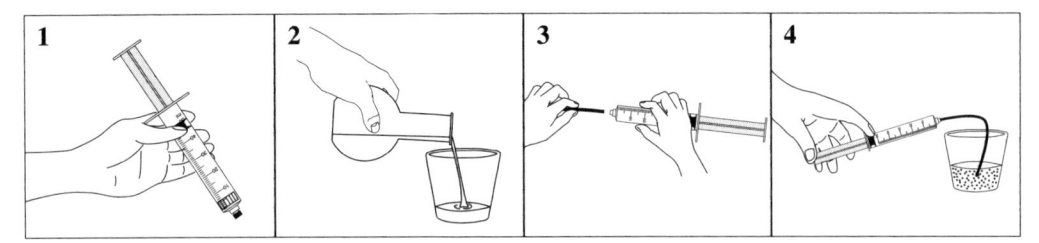

Teacher Notes

1. Use about 15 mL of carbon dioxide gas from Part A for this part of the experiment.

2. Pour 10–15 mL of limewater into a small beaker. Complete the following steps as soon as possible after receiving the limewater. If exposed to air for too long, the limewater will begin to get cloudy.

3. Remove the syringe cap and quickly attach a piece of latex tubing to the syringe.

4. Tilt the syringe and bubble about 10–15 mL of the $CO_2$ gas from the syringe into the limewater. Record your observations in the data table.

### Part C. Carbon Dioxide and pH

1. Use about 45 mL of carbon dioxide gas from Part A for this part of the experiment.

2. Fill a small beaker about half-full with distilled or deionized water.

3. Add about 20 drops (1 mL) of universal indicator to the water and record the initial color and pH in the data table. Set the solution aside. It will be used in Step 5.

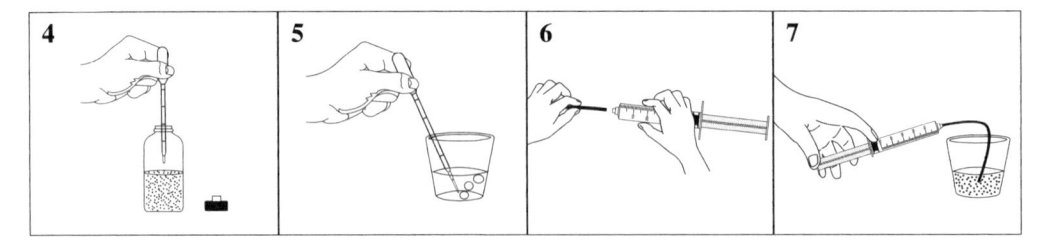

4. Remove the cap from the 6 M ammonium hydroxide solution and collect a pipetful of ammonia gas from above the surface. Do this by emptying and filling the pipet several times above the liquid. *Caution:* Do not remove any of the liquid.

5. Bubble the ammonia vapor through the indicator solution. Record the color and pH of the indicator solution in the data table and set the solution aside again. It will be used in Step 8.

6. Remove the syringe cap and attach a piece of latex tubing to the syringe.

7. Slowly bubble the remaining $CO_2$ gas from the syringe into the universal indicator solution.

Teacher Notes

8. Record the color, the pH of the universal indicator solution, and other observations in the data table.

### Part D.  Reaction of Carbon Dioxide and Sodium Hydroxide

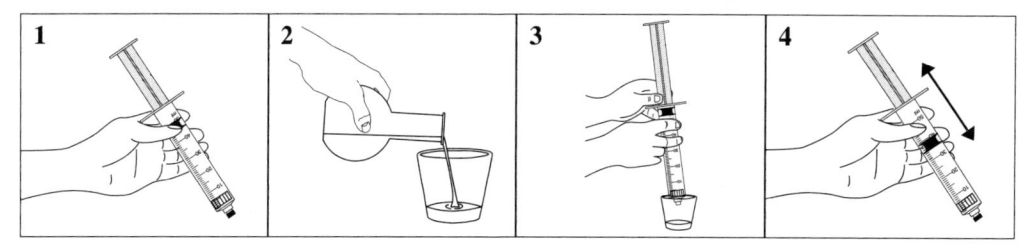

1. Repeat Part A to collect about 45 mL of carbon dioxide gas.

2. Pour about 10 mL of 6 M sodium hydroxide solution into a small beaker.

3. Remove the syringe cap and draw 5 mL of NaOH into the syringe and gently shake the syringe to begin the reaction. Record your observations in the data table.

### Part E.  Does Carbon Dioxide Support Combustion?

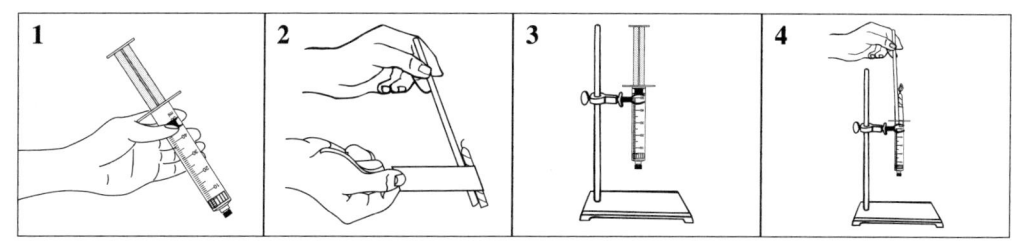

1. Repeat Part A to collect about 60 mL of carbon dioxide gas.

2. Tape a small candle to a glass stirring rod and set the apparatus aside. Make sure the tape is close to the bottom of the candle.

3. Use a ring stand and clamp to hold the syringe in a vertical position with the latex syringe cap in place and the plunger up. Remove the plunger by gently pulling it out of the syringe.

4. Light the candle. Lower the lit candle completely into the syringe barrel using the glass rod and record your observations in the data table. *Caution:* Be careful not to burn your fingers. Allow the glass rod to cool before removing the candle—hot glass looks like cold glass.

# Carbon Dioxide, What a Gas – Page 8

Name: _____

Class/Lab Period: _____

# Carbon Dioxide, What a Gas

## Data Table

|  | Reactants | Observations |
|---|---|---|
| Part A | | |
| Part B | | |
| Part C | | |
| Part D | | |
| Part E | | |

Teacher Notes

**Post-Lab Questions** *(Use a separate sheet of paper to answer the following questions.)*

1. What was observed after adding the carbon dioxide gas to the limewater in Part B?

2. Write the chemical equation for the reaction between carbon dioxide gas and limewater.

3. What was the initial pH of the distilled or deionized water in Part C? Explain.

4. Based on your observations of the universal indicator solution, is ammonia gas soluble in water? Explain.

5. Write the chemical equation for the reaction between dissolved carbon dioxide and ammonia in Part C. *Hint:* Water is one of the reactants.

6. From lab observations, is ammonia an acid or a base? Is carbon dioxide an acid or a base? Explain based on the indicator color changes.

7. What changes were observed in the pressure and volume of carbon dioxide gas in the syringe in Part D?

8. Write the chemical equation for the reaction between carbon dioxide and sodium hydroxide.

9. Solutions of bases such as sodium hydroxide or calcium hydroxide are not stable if they sit in the air for an extended period of time. Based on your observations, suggest a reason for this.

10. What happened to the burning candle in Part E? Could carbon dioxide gas be used as a fire extinguisher?

11. Why was the syringe held upright in Part E? Did the carbon dioxide quickly escape from the syringe?

12. Which gas has a greater density, carbon dioxide or air? How can you tell? *Hint:* Compare the molar masses of oxygen and nitrogen with that of carbon dioxide.

Carbon Dioxide, What a Gas

**Teacher's Notes**

## Teacher's Notes
### Carbon Dioxide, What a Gas

*Microscale*

**Master Materials List** *(for a class of 30 students working in pairs)*

Ammonium hydroxide solution, NH$_4$OH, 6 M, 20 mL (source of ammonia gas)

Hydrochloric acid solution, HCl, 1 M, 500 mL

Limewater, Ca(OH)$_2$, saturated solution, 250 mL

Sodium bicarbonate, NaHCO$_3$, 20 g

Sodium hydroxide solution, NaOH, 6 M, 200 mL

Universal indicator solution, 35 mL

Universal indicator color card, 1

Water

Beakers, 100-mL, 30

Balances, centigram (0.01-g precision), 3

Beral-type pipets, 15

Candles, small, pkg 20

Gas-collecting supplies*

Latex tubing, 6-in piece, 15

Syringes, 60-mL, 15

Syringe tip caps, latex, 15

Vial caps, plastic, 15

Matches

Ring stands with clamps, 15

Silicone grease

Spatulas, 15

Stirring rods, glass, 15

Tape

*The gas-collecting supplies are provided in the "Classroom Equipment Kit" for microscale gas chemistry available from Flinn Scientific (Catalog No. AP5951).

**Preparation of Solutions** *(for a class of 30 students working in pairs)*

*Ammonium Hydroxide, 6 M:* Cool 20 mL of distilled or deionized water in an ice bath and carefully add 20.3 mL of concentrated (14.8 M) ammonium hydroxide. Stir to mix and allow to warm to room temperature, then dilute to 50 mL with water.

*Hydrochloric Acid, 1 M:* Carefully add 83 mL of concentrated hydrochloric acid (12 M) to about 500 mL of distilled or deionized water. Stir to mix and allow to cool to room temperature, then dilute to 1 L with water. *Note:* Always add acid to water.

*Sodium Hydroxide, 6 M:* Cool 100 mL of distilled or deionized water in an ice bath and carefully add 60.0 g of fresh sodium hydroxide pellets. Stir to dissolve and allow to come to room temperature, then dilute to 250 mL with water.

**Safety Precautions**

*Gases in the syringe may be under pressure and could spray liquid chemicals. Follow the instructions and use only the quantities suggested. Ammonium hydroxide and hydrochloric acid solutions are toxic by inhalation and ingestion, and are corrosive to all body tissues. Keep spill control materials on hand to clean up chemical spills. Ammonia fumes can burn nasal membranes; always handle ammonia solutions in an operating fume hood. Sodium hydroxide is a corrosive liquid and is especially dangerous to skin and eyes. Avoid contact of all chemicals with skin and eyes. Wear chemical splash goggles and chemical-resistant gloves and apron. Remind students to wash their hands thoroughly with soap and water before leaving the laboratory. Please review current Material Safety Data Sheets for additional safety, handling, and disposal information.*

*Save valuable time and money by purchasing ready-made solutions. See the Master Materials Guide at the end of this book for catalog numbers.*

# Teacher's Notes

## Disposal

Please consult your current *Flinn Scientific Catalog/Reference Manual* for general guidelines and specific procedures governing the disposal of laboratory waste. Excess carbon dioxide can be released into the air. Excess reagents can be rinsed down the drain with plenty of water according to Flinn Suggested Disposal Method #26b.

## Lab Hints

- The experimental work for this activity may be completed in a standard 50-minute lab period. The students may then complete the *Post-Lab Questions* either outside of class or on a subsequent day. Alternatively, the procedure and questions may be scheduled over a two-day period.

- The limewater provided to students in Part B should be clear. If the stock limewater is agitated and the solution turns cloudy, allow the solution to settle. Decant the solution and use only the clear liquid for the test.

- Demonstrate the procedure for washing carbon dioxide. Washing the gas removes excess hydrochloric acid from the syringe, which could affect the acid–base experiments involving carbon dioxide. Supply a waste beaker at each lab table for the wastewater from the washings.

## Teaching Tips

- Relate the chemistry observed in this experiment to a real-life problem involved in the space program. Carbon dioxide gas is continuously being produced by respiration and exhaled in the breath. If the carbon dioxide is not continuously removed from the air in a closed system, the concentration of carbon dioxide will soon reach toxic levels. The traditional method of removing carbon dioxide in the space shuttle involves reaction with solid lithium hydroxide in special canisters. Assuming that the average production of carbon dioxide by one person over a 24-hour period is 500 L, discuss the stoichiometry calculations for the removal of this amount of $CO_2(g)$ by reaction with LiOH(s).

$$CO_2 + 2LiOH \rightarrow Li_2CO_3 + H_2O$$

$$\text{Moles } CO_2 = 500 \text{ L} \times \frac{1 \text{ mole}}{24.5 \text{ L}} = 20.4 \text{ moles } CO_2 \text{ (at 1 atm pressure and 25 °C)}$$

$$\text{Moles LiOH needed} = 20.4 \text{ moles } CO_2 \times \frac{2 \text{ moles LiOH}}{1 \text{ mole } CO_2} = 40.8 \text{ moles LiOH}$$

$$\text{Moles LiOH needed} = 40.8 \text{ moles} \times \frac{23.95 \text{ g}}{1 \text{ mole}} = 977 \text{ g LiOH}$$

The amount of carbon dioxide generated by one person depends on the weight of the individual, the level of activity, the lung capacity, and the breathing rate.

# Teacher's Notes

- See the following reference for additional information and experiments utilizing microscale "gases in a syringe." Mattson, Bruce; Anderson, Michael; Schwennsen, Cece *Chemistry of Gases: A Microscale Approach;* Flinn Scientific, Batavia, IL (2002).

**Answers to Pre-Lab Questions** *(Student answers will vary.)*

1. Write the balanced chemical equation for the gas-generating reaction in Part A.

    *$HCl(aq) + NaHCO_3(s) \rightarrow NaCl(aq) + H_2O(l) + CO_2(g)$*

2. When 0.22 g of NaHCO$_3$ and 5.0 mL of 1.0 M HCl are used in Part A, which reactant is the limiting reactant? Show all work.

    *The limiting reactant is NaHCO$_3$.*

    $$0.22 \text{ g } NaHCO_3 \times \frac{1 \text{ mole}}{84.01 \text{ g}} = 0.0026 \text{ mole } NaHCO_3 \text{ (limiting reagent)}$$

    $$\frac{1.0 \text{ mole } HCl}{1 \text{ L}} \times 0.0050 \text{ L} = 0.0050 \text{ mole } HCl \text{ (excess reactant)}$$

3. What type of reaction occurs in the syringe in Part A—oxidation–reduction, acid–base, or precipitation?

    *This is an acid–base reaction. HCl is an acid and NaHCO$_3$ is a base.*

# Teacher's Notes

Teacher Notes

## Sample Data

*Student data will vary.*

### Data Table

|  | Reactants | Observations |
|---|---|---|
| Part A | $NaHCO_3(s)$<br>$HCl(aq)$ | Bubbles formed and fizzing occurred.<br>Syringe moved out as gas was produced. |
| Part B | $CO_2$<br>Limewater [$Ca(OH)_2$] | White cloudy precipitate formed in beaker. |
| Part C | $CO_2(g)$<br>Universal indicator<br>$NH_3(g)$ | Water + indicator → light green (pH = 6)<br>Ammonia + indicator → blue (pH = 9)<br>$CO_2$ + indicator → orange (pH = 5) |
| Part D | $CO_2(g)$<br>$NaOH(aq)$ | Syringe plunger was drawn inward as the gas pressure decreased. Internal volume decreased. |
| Part E | $CO_2(g)$<br>Lit candle | Lit candle flame was extinguished in the presence of carbon dioxide gas. |

### Answers to Post-Lab Questions *(Student answers will vary.)*

1. What was observed after adding the carbon dioxide gas to the limewater in Part B?

   *A white precipitate was observed when carbon dioxide gas was bubbled into the limewater.*

2. Write the chemical equation for the reaction between carbon dioxide gas and limewater.

   $CO_2(g) + Ca(OH)_2(aq) \rightarrow CaCO_3(s) + H_2O(l)$

3. What was the initial pH of the distilled or deionized water in Part C? Explain.

   *The indicator color was yellow or light green, corresponding to a pH of about 6. Distilled water is slightly acidic due to dissolved carbon dioxide.*

4. Based on your observations of the universal indicator solution, is ammonia gas soluble in water? Explain.

   *After adding ammonia vapors to the water, the indicator color changed from yellow to a blue-violet. This is evidence that ammonia gas, a weak base, dissolved in water.*

5. Write the chemical equation for the reaction between dissolved carbon dioxide gas and ammonia in Part C. *Hint:* Water is one of the reactants.

   $CO_2(g) + NH_3(g) + H_2O(l) \leftrightarrows NH_4^+(aq) + HCO_3^-(aq)$     Overall Equation

   $CO_2(g) \leftrightarrows CO_2(aq)$

   $CO_2(aq) + H_2O(l) \leftrightarrows H^+(aq) + HCO_3^-(aq)$

   $H^+(aq) + NH_3(g) \leftrightarrows NH_4^+(aq)$

# Teacher's Notes

6. From lab observations, is ammonia an acid or a base? Is carbon dioxide an acid or a base? Explain based on the indicator color changes.

    *The indicator color was blue–violet after ammonia was added, showing that ammonia is a base (pH > 8). After adding carbon dioxide, the indicator color returned to yellow–orange, showing that carbon dioxide is an acid (pH < 6).*

7. What changes were observed in the pressure and volume of carbon dioxide gas in Part D?

    *The pressure and volume of carbon dioxide gas in the syringe decreased. Gas pressure is a result of gas molecules colliding with the container walls. In this experiment, the number of carbon dioxide gas molecules in the syringe decreased because they reacted with the sodium hydroxide. This caused the pressure inside the syringe to rapidly decrease. The greater pressure of the air outside the syringe then "forced" the plunger inward and decreased the volume of the gas in the syringe.*

8. Write the chemical equation for the reaction between carbon dioxide and sodium hydroxide.

    $$CO_2(g) + 2NaOH(aq) \rightarrow Na_2CO_3(s) + H_2O(l)$$

9. Solutions of bases such as sodium hydroxide or calcium hydroxide are not stable if they sit in the air for an extended period of time. Based on your observations, suggest a reason for this.

    *Solutions of sodium hydroxide or other bases are not stable if they sit in the air because they will react with the carbon dioxide in the air to form carbonates.*

10. What happened to the burning candle in Part E? Could carbon dioxide gas be used as a fire extinguisher?

    *The flame went out when exposed to the carbon dioxide. Carbon dioxide does not support combustion and is ideal for use in a fire extinguisher as it quickly extinguishes flames.*

11. Why was the syringe held upright in Part E? Did the carbon dioxide quickly escape from the syringe?

    *Carbon dioxide is more dense than air and the syringe should be placed with the barrel opening in an upright direction. If the syringe were held upside down, the carbon dioxide would quickly flow out of the syringe.*

12. Which gas has a greater density, carbon dioxide or air? How can you tell? *Hint:* Compare the molar masses of oxygen and nitrogen with that of carbon dioxide.

    *Carbon dioxide has a greater density than air. Compare the molar mass of carbon dioxide to the major components of air. Air is mostly nitrogen (MM = 28 g/mol) and oxygen (MM = 32 g/mol) compared to carbon dioxide with a molar mass of 44 g/mol. Since the molar volume of a gas does not depend on the nature of the gas, the density of a gas increases as its molar mass increases.*

**Demonstrations**

Teacher Notes

# Collecting Gases by Water Displacement
## Demonstration Procedure

### Introduction

Gas generator bottles provide an easy way to generate and collect gas samples for demonstration purposes. Specific instructions are provided for generating hydrogen gas and collecting the gas by water displacement.

### Concepts

- Generation of gases
- Water displacement

### Materials

| | |
|---|---|
| Gas generator bottle or filter flask* | Pneumatic trough |
| Two-hole rubber stopper* | Gas collecting bottles or tubes, 3 or 4 |
| Thistle tube* | Rubber tubing |
| Bent glass tubing* | Glass plates |
| Hydrochloric acid, HCl, 3 M, 75 mL | Silicone grease |
| Mossy zinc, Zn, 6 g | Water, tap |

*These components are included in the "Gas Generation Bottle" kit available from Flinn Scientific (Catalog No. AP1558).

### Safety Precautions

*Hydrochloric acid solution is toxic by ingestion and inhalation and is severely corrosive to skin, eyes and other tissues. Hydrogen gas is highly flammable and a severe fire hazard. Exercise extreme caution when testing the gas and keep the gas generator away from flames. Wear chemical splash goggles and chemical-resistant gloves and apron. Please review current Material Safety Data Sheets for additional safety, handling, and disposal information.*

### Procedure

1. Set up the apparatus as shown in Figure 1. Lubricate the glass tubing and thistle tube with silicone grease before inserting into the stopper. Make sure the water level is above the platform in the pneumatic trough. Prepare bottles for collecting gas by water displacement. To do this, fill each gas collecting bottle (or tube) over the brim with tap water, and then cover each with a flat glass plate. At this point, invert two of the bottles into a water-filled pneumatic trough, removing the covers once the openings are under water.

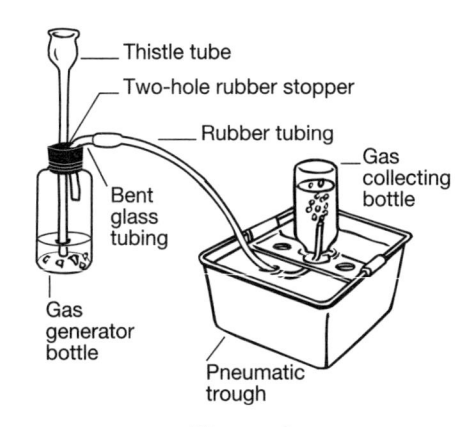

**Figure 1.**

*The water-displacement procedure can also be used to collect oxygen gas generated from the reaction of 6% hydrogen peroxide with a catalyst. In order to collect carbon dioxide gas by water displacement, the water in the collecting bottles should be saturated with carbon dioxide for best results.*

Collecting Gases by Water Displacement

# Demonstrations

Teacher Notes

2. Place about 6 g of mossy zinc into the gas generator bottle and replace the stopper.

3. Check all connections to be sure the gas delivery tube (bent glass tube) leads to the water-filled gas collecting bottle (via rubber tubing and glass tubing).

4. Carefully pour 3 M hydrochloric acid solution through the thistle tube until the acid level in the flask is at least 1 cm above the bottom of the thistle tube. A vigorous reaction with the zinc begins immediately.

5. Allow the gas that evolves to escape into the water of the trough for about 30 seconds to flush out air from the system. Collect three or four bottles of gas by water displacement. As each bottle is filled with gas, lift it from the trough, still inverted, and slip a glass plate over the mouth of the bottle. Place the bottle on the table with the mouth of the bottle down.

6. Use the hydrogen gas in the bottles to demonstrate the properties of hydrogen gas.

## Tips

- Whenever hydrogen gas is generated and tested in the same laboratory, there is a possibility of a tremendous explosion if the testing flames get too near the gas generator. It is suggested that you designate and label the gas generation area as the "No Flames Area" and the hydrogen gas testing area as the "Test Area."

- Add additional acid as needed through the thistle tube to produce the desired quantity of gas. Sulfuric acid may be safely substituted for hydrochloric acid.

- Acid may begin to rise up the thistle tube over the course of the demonstration due to back pressure. Release the pressure by simply loosening the stopper.

- Describe the principles of gas collection by water displacement before beginning the procedure. A gas can be collected if a bottle or tube is filled with water and inverted in a water trough. The water in the bottle or tube will be displaced by the generated gas. As the gas fills the bottle or tube, the water level falls.

- If the glass tubing or thistle tube seems too loose in the stopper and gas seems to be leaking out, seal the connections with silicone grease (or glycerin or Vaseline®).

## Disposal

The gas generator bottle should be carefully disassembled away from any flames. The acid solution may be diluted with water and then neutralized before flushing it down the drain with excess water according to Flinn Suggested Disposal Method #24b. The zinc can be rinsed with water and saved for reuse or disposed of according to Flinn Suggested Disposal Method #26a. Consult your current *Flinn Scientific Catalog/Reference Manual* for general guidelines and specific procedures governing the disposal of laboratory waste.

Flinn ChemTopic™ Labs —Chemistry of Gases

# Demonstrations

Teacher Notes

# Underwater Fireworks
## Chemical Demonstration

### Introduction

Chlorine and acetylene gas are bubbled up inside a large graduated cylinder filled with water. Where the bubbles of the two gases collide, an instantaneous, bright flash of light occurs.

### Concepts

- Chlorine gas
- Acetylene gas
- Chemical properties
- Addition reaction

### Materials

Calcium carbide, $CaC_2$, 2–3 pebble-sized pieces

Hydrochloric acid, HCl, 6 M, 10 mL

Sodium hypochlorite solution (bleach), NaOCl, 100 mL

Flask, Erlenmeyer, 250-mL

Flexible plastic tubing (2–4 mm ID), 10–20 cm

Graduated cylinder or hydrometer, borosilicate glass, 1-L or 2-L

Rubber stopper, 1-hole (to fit 250-mL flask)

Support stand and clamp

Thin glass or plastic tubing (3–5 mm OD)

### Safety Precautions

*Sodium hypochlorite solution is a corrosive liquid and toxic by ingestion; it may cause skin burns. The solution produces chlorine gas when heated or reacted with acid. Hydrochloric acid is highly toxic by ingestion or inhalation and severely corrosive to skin and eyes. Calcium carbide is corrosive to eyes and skin; exposure to water or moisture produces flammable acetylene gas. The reactions in this demonstration release harmful chlorine gas and flammable acetylene gas. Perform the demonstration in an operating fume hood or a well-ventilated room. Wear chemical splash goggles and chemical-resistant gloves and chemical-resistant apron. Please review current Material Safety Data Sheets for additional safety, handling, and disposal information.*

### Preparation

1. Cut a length of glass tubing about 10 cm longer than the height of the graduated cylinder. Cut a second piece of glass tubing about 10 cm in length and carefully insert it into a one-holed rubber stopper. Attach the two pieces of glass tubing with flexible plastic tubing about 10 to 20 cm in length. Insert the long glass tube into the graduated cylinder as shown in the figure on the next page.

2. Fill the graduated cylinder with distilled or deionized water to within 1–2 cm of the top to prevent gases from collecting at the top of the cylinder.

*This demonstration is a favorite of many experienced demonstrators because it is dramatic and a guaranteed crowd pleaser. Even experienced demonstrators, however, sometimes have trouble getting it to work. It is a difficult demonstration to perform. Practice this advanced-level demonstration before performing it for students. Make sure the room is well ventilated!*

## Demonstrations

Teacher Notes

3. Set up a support stand and clamp to hold the 250-mL flask at the appropriate level so that the rubber stopper can easily be connected and removed when the long glass tube is inserted into the graduated cylinder (see setup assembly at the right). Make sure the setup is located in an area with plenty of ventilation to carry away excess chlorine gas, or in a fume hood.

### Procedure

1. Working in an operating fume hood or in a very well-ventilated room, place 100 mL of bleach solution in the 250-mL flask and carefully pour in 10 mL of 6 M HCl. *Caution:* Bleach and hydrochloric acid react to form chlorine gas when the flask is swirled or shaken. Quickly connect the 250-mL flask to the one-holed rubber stopper and clamp the flask in place. Do not use a flask smaller than 250-mL. Do not reopen the flask. Use only the exact quantities of each chemical as mentioned above.

2. Swirl the flask slightly until 2 to 3 bubbles of gas rise up out of the tube in the graduated cylinder.

3. Drop 2–3 pebble-sized pieces of calcium carbide into the water in the graduated cylinder. Note the immediate generation of acetylene gas.

4. Swirl the flask gently and maneuver the glass tube along the bottom of the graduated cylinder to cause the bubbles of chlorine to collide with the bubbles of acetylene. Turn down the lights to enhance the visual impact of the reaction. The reaction will last approximately 30 to 45 seconds. If the calcium carbide is consumed but chlorine gas is still being produced, additional calcium carbide pieces can be added to the cylinder.

5. If not already in a fume hood, move the setup back to the fume hood when the reaction is complete to effectively degas the solutions.

### Disposal

Allow the solutions to ventilate in an operating fume hood for 12–24 hours until all the chlorine gas has evaporated. The degassed bleach/hydrochloric acid solution can go down the drain with excess water according Flinn Suggested Disposal Method #26b. The chlorine water in the graduated cylinder and bleach/hydrochloric acid solution in the Erlenmeyer flask may also be disposed of using Flinn Suggested Disposal Method #12a. Sodium thiosulfate solutions may be disposed of according to Flinn Suggested Disposal Method #12b. Please consult your current *Flinn Scientific Catalog/Reference Manual* for proper disposal procedures.

# Demonstrations

Teacher Notes

## Tips

- Always use fresh sodium hypochlorite to generate chlorine gas.

- Tipping the cylinder a little can facilitate the reaction, for it causes the bubbles to travel up the inside surface of the clyinder, increasing the likelihood that the bubbles will collide with one another.

- If ventilation is a problem, use the following chlorine trap: Place a plastic bag over the mouth of the graduated cylinder, and secure it in place with a rubber band. Poke a hole through one corner of the bag for the glass tube delivering the chlorine gas and one hole in the other corner for a length of tubing to deliver any unreacted chlorine into a beaker filled with 50% aqueous sodium thiosulfate ($Na_2S_2O_3$) solution. This should filter out most of the chlorine. To make a 50% aqueous solution of sodium thiosulfate: Add 50 g of sodium thiosulfate to approximately 50 mL of distilled water. Stir to dissolve the solid (some heating may be required), then dilute the solution to a final volume of 100 mL with distilled water.

- Do not use flexible plastic tubing longer than 20 cm to deliver the chlorine gas. Longer tubing creates more resistance for the flow of gas and may prevent the gas from flowing through the tube smoothly. This may cause a pressure buildup in the flask that may pop the rubber stopper off the top of the flask and release harmful chlorine gas.

- Do not use tap water in this demonstration. The dissolved ions in tap water will interfere with the addition reaction. For best results, use distilled or deionized water.

- To reduce the amount of chlorine gas lost after adding hydrochloric acid to the bleach, attach the flask as quickly as possible to the one-holed rubber stopper. Do not agitate or swirl the flask until the tubing is connected.

- Smaller-sized graduated cylinders or hydrometers may be used. A smaller cylinder will cause the bubbles of chlorine and acetylene to collide more frequently, but the sparks may not be as visible from a distance. Do not use a cylinder smaller than 250-mL.

- "Underwater Fireworks" is available as a chemical demonstration kit from Flinn Scientific (Catalog No. AP8728).

## Discussion

In some hydrocarbons, two or even three pairs of electrons can be shared between two adjacent carbon atoms. These multiple sharings are known as double or triple bonds, and the areas where they occur are said to have high electron densities. Hydrocarbons with double or triple bonds are referred to as "unsaturated." Halogens have seven electrons in their outermost level. Thus, they only need one more electron to form a stable octet. This gives them a high electron affinity. Because of this high affinity for electrons, and the high density of electrons around a multiple bond, halogens will often "attack" (break open and connect onto) a double or triple bond in an unsaturated hydrocarbon.

Underwater Fireworks

# Demonstrations

When chlorine and acetylene gas mix, the electrophilic chlorine attacks the triple bond in acetylene and two competing reactions occur. The predominant reaction is chlorine adding across the carbon–carbon triple bond to produce dichloroethylene. Further addition of chlorine will produce tetrachloroethane. In a competing reaction, chlorine abstracts the hydrogen atom from acetylene to produce HCl and carbon. The carbon is visible as black soot which appears near the top of the cylinder. The reactions for the demonstration are the following:

$$CaC_2(s) + 2H_2O(l) \rightarrow C_2H_2(g) + Ca(OH)_2(aq) \qquad \textit{Acetylene generation}$$

$$NaOCl(aq) + 2HCl(aq) \rightarrow Cl_2(g) + NaCl(aq) + H_2O(l) \qquad \textit{Chlorine generation}$$

$$H\text{—}C\equiv C\text{—}H(g) + Cl_2(g) \rightarrow \underset{\underset{Cl\ \ H}{}}{\overset{\overset{H\ \ Cl}{}}{C=C}}(aq) \qquad \textit{Addition reaction}$$

$$\underset{\underset{Cl\ \ H}{}}{\overset{\overset{H\ \ Cl}{}}{C=C}}(aq) + Cl_2(g) \rightarrow H\text{—}\underset{\underset{Cl\ \ Cl}{}}{\overset{\overset{Cl\ \ Cl}{}}{C\text{—}C}}\text{—}H(aq)$$

$$H\text{—}C\equiv C\text{—}H(g) + Cl_2(g) \rightarrow 2HCl(aq) + 2C(s) \qquad \textit{Abstraction reaction}$$

Activation energy is the energy required by reactant particles so that they will collide with enough force to initiate a reaction. Many reactions, even exothermic reactions such as the combustion of hydrogen or methane, require high temperatures or sparks to initiate the process. This particular reaction between acetylene (an unsaturated hydrocarbon) and chlorine (a halogen) has a low enough activation energy that room temperature is "hot enough" for the reaction to occur spontaneously.

*Teacher Notes*

## Demonstrations

Teacher Notes

# Flaming Vapor Ramp
## Safety Demonstration

### Introduction

Vapors from volatile, flammable liquids are generally heavier than air and can travel along a countertop to an ignition source. Once vapors have been ignited, their flames will quickly follow the vapor trail back to the vapor source and may result in a very large fire or explosion.

### Concepts

- Density of gases
- Flammability
- Fire safety

### Materials

Aluminum angle bracket, 2.5 ft in length*  Match or lighter
Ring stand and clamp  Erlenmeyer flask, 1-L
Hexanes, 3 mL  Stopper, 1-hole, to fit flask
Candle, votive

*Sold commercially in many home improvement stores as an angle bracket for drop ceilings.

### Safety Precautions

*Be very careful while performing this demonstration. Hexanes is a flammable liquid and may be irritating to the respiratory tract. Do not use more hexanes than is specified in the procedure. The flames may become too large and it will also increase the fire hazard should the flask fall and break. Do not substitute a more volatile liquid; many are dangerously combustible and the vapor trail may enter the flask and lead to an explosion. Ether (diethyl ether) or methyl alcohol, for example, are far too volatile to use anywhere near an open flame or ignition source. Wear chemical splash goggles, chemical-resistant gloves, and a chemical-resistant apron. Please review current Material Safety Data Sheets for additional safety, handling, and disposal information.*

### Preparation

1. Clear off a countertop before starting. Remove all combustible materials such as paper from the demonstration area.

2. Prepare a vapor ramp by elevating one end of the aluminum angle bracket using a ring stand and clamp. The ramp should be at a 20° angle or about 20 cm elevation (see Figure 1).

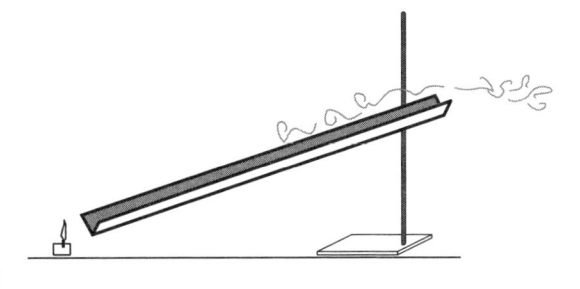

**Figure 1.**

3. Place an unlit candle on the countertop directly below the lower end of the vapor ramp.

4. Pour about 2–3 mL of hexanes into the 1-L Erlenmeyer flask.

5. Place a one-hole stopper on top of the flask and swirl the flask to evaporate the hexanes. Allow the flask to sit for a few minutes to allow hexanes vapors to fill the flask. Set the flask aside.

*"Flaming Vapor Ramp" is available as a Chemical Demonstration Kit from Flinn Scientific (Catalog No. AP6154).*

# Demonstrations

## Procedure

Teacher Notes

1. Have entire class put on their safety goggles.

2. Light the candle and position it so that the flame is even with the bottom of the ramp.

3. Remove the stopper from the flask containing the hexanes. Gradually pour the hexanes *vapors* down the ramp for about 3 seconds. Tip the flask slightly and do NOT allow any liquid to pour out.

4. Be prepared to have the fumes catch fire! After a few seconds, the vapors will ignite and then race up the ramp.

5. The demonstration can be repeated after the flames have extinguished.

## Disposal

Please consult your current *Flinn Scientific Catalog/Reference Manual* for general guidelines and specific procedures governing the disposal of laboratory waste. The hexanes solution may be disposed of according to Flinn Suggested Disposal Method #18a.

## Tips

- Hexane, hexanes, and petroleum ether (NOT ethyl ether) are similar solvents and will work well in the demonstration. *Do not substitute any other flammable liquids.*

- If the ramp cannot be adjusted using a ring stand and clamp, hold the ramp with one hand using an oven glove or a fire-resistant welder's glove. Hold the ramp from beneath, open-side up. Keep fingers and gloves away from any flames.

- Practice this demonstration beforehand to know how long to pour the hexanes vapors. The flask should not be near the trough when the flames ignite. If you are still pouring when the flames start, take the flask away from the top of the vapor ramp to prevent the fire from going back into it. If the flame does make it back into the flask, it will burn for a while at the mouth of the flask—there is not enough oxygen inside the flask for the entire sample to burn.

## Discussion

Many organic solvents have low boiling points and are highly volatile at ambient temperatures. For example, the hexanes solution has a boiling point of 68–70 °C and a vapor pressure of 150 mm Hg at 25 °C. Most organic vapors are colorless gases and therefore nearly impossible to see. Hexane ($C_6H_{14}$) has a molecular weight of 86 g/mol. The density of hexane vapors is nearly three times that of air. Thus hexanes vapors (and most other organic vapors) are heavier than air and will sink in air. Heavier-than-air vapors are also easy to pour. When the hexane vapors are poured down the vapor ramp and make their way to the lit candle, all three necessary ingredients for a fire are present—air containing oxygen, hexane fuel, and a source of ignition or heat. The flames travel back up the ramp, leaving an impressive trail of fire in the path. This is an especially valuable demonstration because of the safety lesson it conveys. Using flammable liquids indoors can be a fire hazard even if you are nowhere near an open flame. As any firefighter can attest, volatile fumes can travel along the floor, even down steps, and find an ignition source, such as the pilot light of a furnace or hot water heater or an electric switch. Ignition sources are less common outdoors, and winds generally cause the fumes to dissipate before they reach combustible levels.

*"Hexanes" is a flammable but nontoxic mixture of n-hexane and other $C_6H_{14}$ isomers. Petroleum ether **(not diethyl ether)** is also a mixture of lightweight, predominantly $C_6$-hydrocarbons.*

Flinn ChemTopic™ Labs —Chemistry of Gases

Teacher Notes

# The Collapsing Bottle
## A Carbon Dioxide Demonstration

### Introduction

Completely collapse a two-liter soda bottle using chemicals! Simply fill the bottle with carbon dioxide gas, add sodium hydroxide, and observe as the bottle gets hot and completely crushes inward.

### Concepts

- Carbon dioxide gas
- Gas solubility
- Acid–base reaction
- Atmospheric pressure

### Materials

Soda bottle, 2-L, empty PETE* (polyethylene terephthalate) bottle
Sodium hydroxide, NaOH, 6 M, 30 mL
Carbon dioxide ($CO_2$) gas cylinder
   or
Carbon dioxide gas generator:    Sodium bicarbonate
                                         Hydrochloric acid (3 M or higher)
                                         Gas generator setup

*To identify a PETE bottle, look for a triangle with a "1" on the bottom.

### Safety Precautions

*Sodium hydroxide solution is a corrosive liquid; avoid all body tissue contact. Do not reuse the 2-liter soda bottle—strong bases will decompose PETE bottles over time. Wear chemical splash goggles, chemical-resistant gloves, and a chemical-resistant apron. Please review current Material Safety Data Sheets for additional safety, handling, and disposal information.*

### Preparation

Fill a clean, empty 2-L polyethylene terephthalate (PETE) soda bottle with carbon dioxide gas ($CO_2$) from either a refillable gas cylinder or a lecture bottle. Alternatively, generate carbon dioxide gas in a gas-generating bottle and collect the gas in a soda bottle. To generate carbon dioxide in the lab, add sodium bicarbonate or calcium carbonate to 6 M hydrochloric acid in a 500-mL Erlenmeyer flask equipped with a one-hole stopper and a glass tube connected to plastic tubing. As soon as the bicarbonate is added, place the stopper on the flask and the plastic tube in the 2-L soda bottle to collect the carbon dioxide. Carbon dioxide is approximately 1.5 times heavier than air. Keep the soda bottle upright and fill from the bottom up, then cap the bottle.

## Procedure

1. Remove the cap from the 2-L soda bottle, add approximately 30 mL of 6 M NaOH, and quickly reseal the bottle. Shake the bottle once and it will immediately collapse.

2. Vigorously shake the bottle and it will completely collapse until the sides are touching. The heat generated by the exothermic reaction can be felt through the walls of the bottle.

3. Allow the collapsed bottle to sit overnight. By the next morning, large crystals of sodium carbonate will have formed.

## Disposal

Consult your current *Flinn Scientific Catalog/Reference Manual* for general guidelines and specific procedures governing the disposal of laboratory waste. The final waste solution may be flushed down the drain with excess water according to Flinn Suggested Disposal Method #26b. The soda bottle may be rinsed out and disposed of in the trash.

## Tips

- The importance of surface area in gas–liquid reactions can be shown by performing this demonstration in two identical bottles. Shake one bottle, creating greater gas–liquid surface area contact, and let the other bottle sit without shaking. The shaken bottle will collapse much quicker.

- Solid sodium hydroxide pellets will work but require much longer reaction times than sodium hydroxide solutions.

## Discussion

Carbon dioxide is a slightly acidic gas that readily dissolves in water to produce carbonic acid (Equation 1). Carbonic acid neutralizes the sodium hydroxide added to the bottle (Equation 2). The net result is the conversion of gaseous carbon dioxide to an aqueous solution of sodium carbonate. As the amount of carbon dioxide decreases, the pressure inside the soda bottle decreases while the atmospheric pressure on the outside remains the same, leading to a collapsing bottle. The reaction of carbon dioxide with sodium hydroxide is often used to trap carbon dioxide gas in laboratory experiments.

$$CO_2(g) + H_2O(l) \rightleftharpoons H_2CO_3(aq) \qquad \text{Equation 1}$$

$$H_2CO_3(aq) + 2NaOH(aq) \rightarrow Na_2CO_3(aq) + 2H_2O(l) \qquad \text{Equation 2}$$

Although the equilibrium represented by Equation 1 lies far to the left, it is shifted to the right by the neutralization of the product with sodium hydroxide, according to LeChâtlier's Principle. As a result, all of the carbon dioxide gas is consumed and the bottle collapses.

# Demonstrations

Teacher Notes

# Solubility of Carbon Dioxide
## Dry Ice Color Show

### Introduction

Add a small piece of solid carbon dioxide to a colored indicator solution and watch as the solution immediately begins to "boil" and change color.

### Concepts

- Carbon dioxide gas
- Sublimation
- Acid–base indicators

### Materials

Ammonia, household, $NH_3$, 5 mL  
Beakers, 1-L, 5  
Beakers, 100-mL, 5  
Dry ice nuggets, 5–10  
Gloves, insulated type  
Water, distilled or deionized  
Wood splint (optional)

Indicator solutions  
    Bromcresol green, 0.04% aqueous, 2 mL  
    Bromthymol blue, 0.04% aqueous, 2 mL  
    Methyl red, 0.02% aqueous, 2 mL  
    Phenol red, 0.02% aqueous, 2 mL  
    Universal indicator, 2 mL

### Safety Precautions

*Dry ice (solid carbon dioxide) is an extremely cold solid (–78.5 °C) and will cause frostbite. Do not touch dry ice to bare skin; always handle with proper gloves. Household ammonia is slightly toxic by ingestion and inhalation; the vapor is irritating, especially to the eyes. Universal indicator solution contains alcohol and is therefore flammable. Wear chemical splash goggles, chemical-resistant gloves, and a chemical-resistant apron. Please review current Material Safety Data Sheets for additional safety, handling, and disposal information.*

### Preparation

1. Set five 1-L beakers in clear view on a demonstration table.
2. Fill each with approximately 750 mL of distilled water (about ¾ full).
3. Add 2 mL of indicator to the water in the beakers, in the following order:

| Beaker | Indicator | Basic Color | Acidic Color | pH Range |
|---|---|---|---|---|
| 1 | Bromcresol green | Blue | Yellow-green | 5.4 to 3.8 |
| 2 | Universal indicator | Purple | Orange | 10 to 4 |
| 3 | Phenol red | Red | Yellow | 8.4 to 6.8 |
| 4 | Methyl red | Yellow | Red | 6.2 to 4.4 |
| 5 | Bromthymol blue | Blue | Yellow | 7.6 to 6.0 |

Each indicator should begin in the basic range and change to the acidic range upon addition of dry ice. The color changes from basic to acidic are shown in the table.

*Tall-form beakers or hydrometer cylinders give a nice presentation in this demonstration. "Dry Ice Color Show" is available as a chemical demonstration kit from Flinn Scientific (Catalog No. AP6201).*

Solubility of Carbon Dioxide

# Demonstrations

Teacher Notes

4. To the beakers containing universal indicator and bromthymol blue, add 1 mL of household ammonia.

5. The indicator solutions should now all be in their basic color range. If they are not, add ammonia dropwise to obtain the basic color as indicated in the table. Avoid adding excess ammonia or the colors will take too long to change when dry ice is added.

6. Set up reference solutions in the five 100-mL beakers by pouring approximately 70 mL from each large beaker into its corresponding small beaker. Set the reference beakers next to their corresponding large beakers.

## Procedure

1. Use insulated gloves to add one or two nuggets of dry ice to each beaker of basic indicator solution. The dry ice immediately begins to sublime. Vigorous bubbling occurs and a heavy white vapor appears. Shortly afterwards, each indicator solution changes color to its acidic color (see table on page 59).

2. Have students make observations about the temperature of the solutions and of the vapor. Have students feel the sides of the beakers. Notice that the vapor is cool (rather than hot) to the touch, as are the water solutions. Explain to the students that "boiling" does not always occur at high temperature—a common misconception—and that the solution is not actually boiling. The solution appears to be boiling because there is such a large temperature difference between the water and the dry ice.

3. *(Optional)* Take a burning or glowing splint and place it in the vapor. The flame will be extinguished due to the carbon dioxide gas.

## Disposal

Please consult your current *Flinn Scientific Catalog/Reference Manual* for general guidelines and specific procedures governing the disposal of laboratory waste. All materials may be disposed of according to Flinn Suggested Disposal Method #26b. Extra dry ice may be placed in a well-ventilated area and allowed to sublime.

## Tips

- The indicator solutions in the beakers can be reused from class to class by adding a small amount of household ammonia, dropwise, after the demonstration is complete. Care must be taken not to make the solutions too basic or else the color changes will not occur.

- Slabs of dry ice can be broken or cracked using a hammer. Wrap the dry ice slab in a towel or place in a zipper-lock bag before striking it with a hammer. Dry ice may be obtained from a local ice cream store or ice company. Look in your local Yellow Pages under ice or dry ice. Dry ice costs vary from about $8.00 to $13.00 per 10 lbs, but some sources may supply it free for educational purposes. Dry ice may also be made using the Dry Ice Maker, Flinn Catalog No. AP4416.

- If the prepared indicator solutions sit in the open air for too long (especially the phenol red), they will begin to change color as carbon dioxide from the air dissolves in the solution, making it acidic. Adding slightly more ammonia will change the solutions back to their basic color.

*Flinn ChemTopic™ Labs* —Chemistry of Gases

# Demonstrations

Teacher Notes

- If distilled or deionized water is not available, use tap water. Be sure to adjust the pH appropriately as some tap water does not have a neutral pH.

- Try other indicators that change color at a pH of near neutral, such as neutral red (yellow to red, 8.0 to 6.8) and bromcresol purple (purple to yellow, 6.8 to 5.2).

- Use the universal indicator overhead color chart (AP5367) to follow pH changes in the universal indicator solution.

## Discussion

Dry ice is solid carbon dioxide ($CO_2$). The temperature of dry ice is –78.5 °C (or –109.3 °F), making it extremely cold to the touch. Carbon dioxide is normally found in the gaseous state, making up approximately 0.04% of our atmosphere. It is a colorless, odorless, noncombustible gas with a faint acid taste. Dry ice is made by cooling atmospheric air and compressing the solid into desired forms, such as blocks, nuggets, pucks, etc. The different gases that make up atmospheric air (nitrogen, oxygen, etc.) condense at different temperatures, and therefore may be easily separated. Carbon dioxide forms a frosty, white solid at –78.5 °C. As a solid, carbon dioxide can cause frostbite on contact with skin and will stick to moist tissue (such as wet skin or your tongue). Solid carbon dioxide undergoes sublimation upon exposure to air. This means it transforms directly from the solid phase to the gaseous phase without melting to a liquid.

When dry ice is placed in water (as in this demonstration), it sublimes rapidly since the water is so much warmer than the dry ice. The solution appears to boil. As the dry ice sublimes to gaseous $CO_2$, some of the gas bubbles away quickly and some dissolves in the water. A heavy white cloud of condensed water vapor forms above the liquid (due to the coldness of the escaping $CO_2$ gas). As the $CO_2$ gas dissolves in the water, the solution becomes more acidic from the production of carbonic acid ($H_2CO_3$), a weak acid, according to the following equation:

$$H_2O(l) + CO_2(g) \rightleftarrows H_2CO_3(aq)$$

The indicators change to their acidic forms as the pH levels of the solutions drop, producing a color change. The time required for the change to occur depends on the initial pH of the solution, the transition point of the indicator, and how much dry ice was added to the solution.

## Supplementary Information

This demonstration illustrates the sublimation of dry ice—the conversion of carbon dioxide directly from the solid state to the gaseous state. Liquid carbon dioxide cannot be observed at atmospheric pressure. It is possible, however, to obtain carbon dioxide in the liquid state, that is, to observe the melting of dry ice, by warming the dry ice in a closed system. Consider the following simple experiment.

1. Place a small nugget of dry ice in the bulb of a jumbo plastic pipet.

2. Fold over the stem of the pipet, clamp it firmly using a pair of heavy-duty pliers, and place the pipet bulb into a plastic cup half-filled with water.

# Demonstrations

Teacher Notes

3. As the dry ice warms up, it is converted to gaseous carbon dioxide. The pressure inside the pipet increases due to the buildup of carbon dioxide gas in the closed system. When the internal pressure reaches 5.2 atm, the dry ice melts and then boils!

The triple point of carbon dioxide occurs at a temperature of –57 °C and a pressure of 5.2 atm. This is the point at which all three phases of a substance (solid, liquid, and gas) exist together at equilibrium. For any given substance, there is one and only one specific temperature and specific pressure point at which this can happen.

Note the safety precautions implicit in the experimental procedure described above.

- The dry ice is contained in a small, soft, plastic container. When the container is pressurized, it may explode, but if it does, the explosion will be minimal (although you will get wet).

- The pipet bulb is placed in a plastic cup of water, which serves as a heat sink and also keeps the bulb soft and supple.

**Demonstrations**

Teacher Notes

# Solubility of Ammonia
## Indicator Color Show

### Introduction

Ammonia gas is easily generated by heating concentrated ammonium hydroxide solution. In this demonstration, ammonia gas will be collected in jumbo pipet bulbs and its solubility and acid–base properties will be investigated. Surprise your students with the resulting beautiful indicator color show.

### Concepts

- Ammonia gas
- Acid–base reactions
- Gas solubility
- Indicators

### Materials

Acid–base indicator solutions, 2 mL each
   Bromthymol blue, 0.04%
   Phenolphthalein, 0.5%
   Phenol red, 0.02%
   Thymolphthalein, 0.04%
   Universal indicator
Ammonium hydroxide concentrated solution, $NH_4OH$, 14.8 M, 1 mL
pH Chart showing indicator color changes (optional)
Commercial ammonia cleaning solution (optional)

Beakers, 100-mL, 6
Hot plate
Microtip pipet
Super jumbo pipet bulbs, 5
Tap water

### Safety Precautions

*Concentrated ammonium hydroxide solution is moderately toxic by ingestion and inhalation. It is a serious respiratory hazard; both the liquid and the vapor are extremely irritating, especially to the eyes. Dispense ammonium hydroxide in a hood and perform this demonstration in a well-ventilated lab only. Wear chemical splash goggles and chemical-resistant gloves and apron. Please review current Material Safety Data Sheets for additional safety, handling, and disposal information.*

### Procedure

1. Cut off the stems from five jumbo pipets, leaving about 1 cm of stem attached to the bulb of the pipet. The jumbo pipet bulbs will be used as gas collection vessels.

2. Fill five beakers half full with cold water and add 1–2 mL of a different acid–base indicator (see the *Materials* section) to each beaker. Observe and record the initial color of each indicator solution in cold water.

---

*Vary the amount of indicator added in step 2 depending on the concentration of the indicator solution. Add enough indicator to produce vivid color changes. Phenol red indicator is a very dilute solution—use about 10 mL of this indicator.*

# Demonstrations

Teacher Notes

3. Squeeze the microtip pipet to push out the air and place the pipet tip into the concentrated ammonium hydroxide solution. Draw up enough ammonium hydroxide solution to fill the bulb about one-half full. The microtip pipet serves as the gas generator in this demonstration. *Note:* Remove the pipet from the ammonia solution before completely releasing the bulb. Air, not liquid, must be in the stem of the pipet (otherwise concentrated ammonium hydroxide solution may squirt out of the pipet when the solution is heated). Tap the pipet bulb to remove any liquid, if necessary, from the pipet stem.

4. Insert the microtip pipet containing ammonium hydroxide solution into the cut-off bulb of a jumbo pipet.

5. Fill a 100-mL beaker about one-half full with tap water and heat the water on a hot plate at a medium setting. Place the microtip pipet with its stem up into the hot water bath. Observe the vigorous bubbling of the ammonium hydroxide solution—warming the solution releases ammonia gas.

6. Collect ammonia gas in the super jumbo pipet bulb: Squeeze the bulb to remove as much air as possible. As ammonia gas is formed, slowly release the pressure on the bulb and allow the gas to fill the pipet bulb.

7. Place the tip of the jumbo pipet bulb into one of the beakers filled with cold water and an acid–base indicator (step 1). Gently squeeze the pipet bulb to push out one bubble of gas and allow a drop of water to enter the pipet bulb. *(Observe that the pipet bulb immediately fills with water—the solubility of ammonia gas in water is extremely high. As the ammonia gas pressure inside the bulb rapidly decreases, more water is drawn into the pipet bulb due to the pressure difference with the atmosphere.)*

8. Observe and record the color of the acid–base indicator solution in the jumbo pipet bulb.

9. Repeat steps 6–8 with the remaining acid–base indicator solutions. Collect ammonia gas in a fresh jumbo pipet bulb each time. It should not be necessary to add more ammonium hydroxide solution to the gas-generating pipet. Observe and record the indicator color in each pipet bulb. *(See the table in the Discussion section.)*

10. Write the equation for ammonia gas dissolving in water and the resulting ionization of water to produce "$NH_4OH$." Discuss the evidence from this demonstration that this is a reversible reaction and that ammonia is a weak base.

11. *(Optional)* Read the warning on a container of a commercial cleaner that contains ammonia as the active ingredient. Discuss the significance of the hazard warning. *(The label will probably say do not breathe the vapors and keep off the skin. Ammonia cleaners will release enough ammonia gas at room temperature that breathing the vapors is very dangerous—the gas dissolves in the moisture of the mucous membrane and the lungs. As with any base, ammonia is also a skin irritant.)*

12. *(Optional)* Show students a chart showing the pH range of different indicators and their color changes. Ask students to predict, using the observations from this lab, whether other indicators such as bromcresol green or alizarin would be suitable for this demonstration. Why or why not?

Flinn ChemTopic™ Labs —Chemistry of Gases

# Demonstrations

Teacher Notes

## Disposal

Consult your current *Flinn Scientific Catalog/Reference Manual* for general guidelines and specific procedures governing the disposal of laboratory waste. The indicator solutions may be disposed of down the drain with plenty of excess water according to Flinn Suggested Disposal Method #26b.

## Tips

- Other indicators that give suitable color changes are alizarin, alizarin red, and cresol red.

- If ammonia leaks into a beaker containing an indicator solution and causes a color change, add a few drops of vinegar or dilute acetic acid to change the indicator back to its acidic form.

## Discussion

There is a dual equilibrium which appears to exist when ammonia gas dissolves in water. The fact that ammonia gas is easily driven off when the concentrated ammonia solution is heated suggests a simple solubility equilibrium (Equation 1) to give hydrated ammonia molecules, $NH_3(aq)$.

$$NH_3(g) \rightleftharpoons NH_3(aq) \qquad \qquad \textit{Equation 1}$$

The indicator color changes, however, reveal that the resulting aqueous ammonia solution is basic. The acid–base reaction of ammonia with water is shown in Equation 2.

$$NH_3(aq) + H_2O(l) \rightleftharpoons NH_4^+(aq) + OH^-(aq) \qquad \qquad \textit{Equation 2}$$

The solubility of ammonia gas in water is extremely high—approximately 400 liters of ammonia gas will dissolve in one liter of water at room temperature! As with any gas, the solubility of ammonia gas in water decreases as the temperature increases.

The following table summarizes the pH ranges for the indicators used in this demonstration and their corresponding color changes. Notice that the initial colors of many of the indicators are in the acidic range (pH <7). The pH of water is usually slightly acidic due to the presence of dissolved carbon dioxide.

| Indicator | pH range | Acidic Color | Basic Color |
| --- | --- | --- | --- |
| Bromthymol blue | 6.0–7.6 | Yellow | Blue |
| Phenol Red | 6.8–8.4 | Yellow | Red |
| Phenolphthalein | 8.2–10.0 | Colorless | Red violet |
| Thymolphthalein | 9.3–10.5 | Colorless | Blue |
| Universal Indicator | 4–10 | See chart | See chart |

*The solubility of ammonia gas in water is about 90 g per 100 mL at 0 °C and about 32 g per 100 mL at 25 °C. The room temperature solubility corresponds to a volume of 460 L ammonia gas dissolving in 1 L of water.*

Solubility of Ammonia

# Safety and Disposal Guidelines

## Safety Guidelines

Teachers owe their students a duty of care to protect them from harm and to take reasonable precautions to prevent accidents from occurring. A teacher's duty of care includes the following:

- Supervising students in the classroom.
- Providing adequate instructions for students to perform the tasks required of them.
- Warning students of the possible dangers involved in performing the activity.
- Providing safe facilities and equipment for the performance of the activity.
- Maintaining laboratory equipment in proper working order.

## Safety Contract

The first step in creating a safe laboratory environment is to develop a safety contract that describes the rules of the laboratory for your students. Before a student ever sets foot in a laboratory, the safety contract should be reviewed and then signed by the student and a parent or guardian. Please contact Flinn Scientific at 800-452-1261 or visit the Flinn Website at www.flinnsci.com to request a free copy of the Flinn Scientific Safety Contract.

To fulfill your duty of care, observe the following guidelines:

1. **Be prepared.** Practice all experiments and demonstrations beforehand. Never perform a lab activity if you have not tested it, if you do not understand it, or if you do not have the resources to perform it safely.

2. **Set a good example.** The teacher is the most visible and important role model. Wear your safety goggles whenever you are working in the lab, even (or especially) when class is not in session. Students learn from your good example—whether you are preparing reagents, testing a procedure, or performing a demonstration.

3. **Maintain a safe lab environment.** Provide high-quality goggles that offer adequate protection and are comfortable to wear. Make sure there is proper safety equipment in the laboratory and that it is maintained in good working order. Inspect all safety equipment on a regular basis to ensure its readiness.

4. **Start with safety.** Incorporate safety into each laboratory exercise. Begin each lab period with a discussion of the properties of the chemicals or procedures used in the experiment and any special precautions—including goggle use—that must be observed. Pre-lab assignments are an ideal mechanism to ensure that students are prepared for lab and understand the safety precautions. Record all safety instruction in your lesson plan.

5. **Proper instruction.** Demonstrate new or unusual laboratory procedures before every activity. Instruct students on the safe way to handle chemicals, glassware, and equipment.

# Safety and Disposal

6. **Supervision.** Never leave students unattended—always provide adequate supervision. Work with school administrators to make sure that class size does not exceed the capacity of the room or your ability to maintain a safe lab environment. Be prepared and alert to what students are doing so that you can prevent accidents before they happen.

7. **Understand your resources.** Know yourself, your students, and your resources. Use discretion in choosing experiments and demonstrations that match your background and fit within the knowledge and skill level of your students and the resources of your classroom. You are the best judge of what will work or not. Do not perform any activities that you feel are unsafe, that you are uncomfortable performing, or that you do not have the proper equipment for.

## Safety Precautions

*Specific safety precautions have been written for every experiment and demonstration in this book. The safety information describes the hazardous nature of each chemical and the specific precautions that must be followed to avoid exposure or accidents. The safety section also alerts you to potential dangers in the procedure or techniques. Regardless of what lab program you use, it is important to maintain a library of current Material Safety Data Sheets for all chemicals in your inventory. Please consult current MSDS for additional safety, handling, and disposal information.*

## Disposal Procedures

The disposal procedures included in this book are based on the Suggested Laboratory Chemical Disposal Procedures found in the *Flinn Scientific Catalog/Reference Manual*. The disposal procedures are only suggestions—do not use these procedures without first consulting with your local government regulatory officials.

Many of the experiments and demonstrations produce small volumes of aqueous solutions that can be flushed down the drain with excess water. Do not use this procedure if your drains empty into groundwater through a septic system or into a storm sewer. Local regulations may be more strict on drain disposal than the practices suggested in this book and in the *Flinn Scientific Catalog/Reference Manual*. You must determine what types of disposal procedures are permitted in your area—contact your local authorities.

Any suggested disposal method that includes "discard in the trash" requires your active attention and involvement. Make sure that the material is no longer reactive, is placed in a suitable container (plastic bag or bottle), and is in accordance with local landfill regulations. Please do not inadvertently perform any extra "demonstrations" due to unpredictable chemical reactions occurring in your trash can. Think before you throw!

Finally, please read all the narratives before you attempt any Suggested Laboratory Chemical Disposal Procedure found in your current *Flinn Scientific Catalog/Reference Manual*.

Flinn Scientific is your most trusted and reliable source of reference, safety, and disposal information for all chemicals used in the high school science lab. To request a complimentary copy of the most recent *Flinn Scientific Catalog/Reference Manual,* call us at 800-452-1261 or visit our Web site at www.flinnsci.com.

# National Science Education Standards

## Experiments and Demonstrations

| Content Standards | Common Gases | Preparing and Testing Hydrogen Gas | Oxygen, What a Flame | Carbon Dioxide, What a Gas | Collecting Gases by Water Displacement | Underwater Fireworks | Flaming Vapor Ramp | The Collapsing Bottle | Solubility of Carbon Dioxide | Solubility of Ammonia |
|---|---|---|---|---|---|---|---|---|---|---|
| **Unifying Concepts and Processes** | | | | | | | | | | |
| Systems, order, and organization | | | | | | | | | | |
| Evidence, models, and explanation | ✓ | ✓ | ✓ | ✓ | | ✓ | ✓ | ✓ | ✓ | ✓ |
| Constancy, change, and measurement | | | | | | | | | | |
| Evolution and equilibrium | | | | | | | | | | |
| Form and function | | | | | | | | | | |
| **Science as Inquiry** | | | | | | | | | | |
| Identify questions and concepts that guide scientific investigation | | | | | | | | | | |
| Design and conduct scientific investigations | ✓ | ✓ | ✓ | ✓ | | ✓ | ✓ | ✓ | ✓ | ✓ |
| Use technology and mathematics to improve scientific investigations | | | | | | | | | | |
| Formulate and revise scientific explanations and models using logic and evidence | | | | | | | | | | |
| Recognize and analyze alternative explanations and models | | | | | | | | | | |
| Communicate and defend a scientific argument | | | | | | | | | | |
| Understand scientific inquiry | | | | | | | | | | |
| **Physical Science** | | | | | | | | | | |
| Structure of atoms | | | | | | | | | | |
| Structure and properties of matter | ✓ | ✓ | ✓ | ✓ | ✓ | ✓ | ✓ | ✓ | ✓ | ✓ |
| Chemical reactions | ✓ | ✓ | ✓ | ✓ | ✓ | ✓ | ✓ | ✓ | ✓ | ✓ |
| Motions and forces | | | | | | | | | | |
| Conservation of energy and the increase in disorder | | | | | | | | | | |
| Interactions of energy and matter | | | | | | | | | | |

Flinn ChemTopic™ Labs — Chemistry of Gases

## National Science Education Standards

### Content Standards (continued)

| | Common Gases | Preparing and Testing Hydrogen Gas | Oxygen, What a Flame | Carbon Dioxide, What a Gas | Collecting Gases by Water Displacement | Underwater Fireworks | Flaming Vapor Ramp | The Collapsing Bottle | Solubility of Carbon Dioxide | Solubility of Ammonia |
|---|---|---|---|---|---|---|---|---|---|---|
| **Science and Technology** | | | | | | | | | | |
| Identify a problem or design an opportunity | | | | | | | | | | |
| Propose designs and choose between alternative solutions | | | | | | | | | | |
| Implement a proposed solution | | | | | | | | | | |
| Evaluate the solution and its consequences | | | | | | | | | | |
| Communicate the problem, process, and solution | | | | | | | | | | |
| Understand science and technology | | | | | | | | | | |
| **Science in Personal and Social Perspectives** | | | | | | | | | | |
| Personal and community health | | | | | | | ✓ | | | |
| Population growth | | | | | | | | | | |
| Natural resources | | | | | | | | | | |
| Environmental quality | | | | ✓ | | | | | | |
| Natural and human-induced hazards | ✓ | ✓ | ✓ | ✓ | | | ✓ | | | |
| Science and technology in local, national, and global challenges | | | | ✓ | | | | | | |
| **History and Nature of Science** | | | | | | | | | | |
| Science as a human endeavor | ✓ | ✓ | ✓ | ✓ | | | | | | |
| Nature of scientific knowledge | ✓ | ✓ | ✓ | ✓ | | | | | | |
| Historical perspectives | ✓ | ✓ | ✓ | ✓ | | | | ✓ | | |

## Master Materials Guide

*(for a class of 30 students working in pairs)*

**Experiments and Demonstrations**

| Chemicals | Flinn Scientific Catalog No. | Common Gases | Preparing and Testing Hydrogen Gas | Oxygen, What a Flame | Carbon Dioxide, What a Gas | Collecting Gases by Water Displacement | Underwater Fireworks | Flaming Vapor Ramp | The Collapsing Bottle | Solubility of Carbon Dioxide | Solubility of Ammonia |
|---|---|---|---|---|---|---|---|---|---|---|---|
| Ammonia, household | A0038 | | | | | | | | | 5 mL | |
| Ammonium chloride | A0266 | 2 g | | | | | | | | | |
| Ammonium hydroxide, 14.8 M | A0174 | | | | | | | | | | 2 mL |
| Ammonium hydroxide solution, 6 M | A0192 | | | | 20 mL | | | | | | |
| Bromcresol green indicator solution, 0.04% | B0064 | | | | | | | | | 2 mL | |
| Bromthymol blue indicator solution, 0.04% | B0173 | | | | | | | | | 2 mL | 2 mL |
| Calcium carbide | C0346 | | | | | 2-3 pcs. | | | | | |
| Carbon dioxide | LB1005 | | | | | | | | 1 | | |
| Cleaner, dishwashing | C0241 | 30 mL | | | | | | | | | |
| Copper, foil, (0.005 inches thick) | C0137 | 1 | | | | | | | | | |
| Dextrose | D0002 | | | 19 g | | | | | | | |
| Hexanes* | H0046 | | | | | | | 100 mL | | | |
| Hydrochloric acid solution, 6 M | H0033 | | | | | 10 mL | | | | | |
| Hydrochloric acid solution, 3 M | H0034 | 100 mL | 300 mL | | | | | | | | |
| Hydrochloric acid solution, 1 M | H0013 | | | | 500 mL | | | | | | |
| Hydrogen peroxide solution, 6% | H0029 | | | 1 L | | | | | | | |
| Hydrogen peroxide solution, 3% | H0009 | 100 mL | | | | | | | | | |
| Limewater, saturated solution | L0021 | | | | 250 mL | 250 mL | | | | | |
| Magnesium metal ribbon | M0139 | 30 cm | | | | | | | | | |
| Manganese dioxide | M0023 | 2 g | | | | | | | | | |
| Methyl red indicator solution, 0.02% | M0159 | | | | | | | | | 2 mL | |
| Methylene blue solution, 1% | M0074 | | | 3 mL | | | | | | | |
| Nitric acid solution, 6 M | N0049 | 50 mL | | | | | | | | | |
| Phenolphthalein indicator solution, 1% | P0019 | | | | | | | | | | 2 mL |
| Phenol red indicator solution, 0.02% | P0100 | | | | | | | | | 2 mL | 2 mL |
| Potassium hydroxide | P0058 | | | 15 g | | | | | | | |
| Potassium iodide | P0066 | | | 10 g | | | | | | | |
| Sodium bicarbonate | S0042 | 1 g | | | 20 g | | | | | | |
| Sodium hydroxide solution, 6 M | S0242 | | | | 200 mL | | | | | 30 mL | |
| Sodium hydroxide solution, 3 M | S0447 | 25 mL | | | | | | | | | |
| Sodium hypochlorite solution | S0079 | | | | | | | 100 mL | | | |
| Steel wool | S0128 | | 1 | | | | | | | | |

*Hexanes are included in AP6154, Flaming Vapor Ramp Kit.

*Continued on next page*

# Master Materials Guide

*(for a class of 30 students working in pairs)*            **Experiments and Demonstrations**

| | Flinn Scientific Catalog No. | Common Gases | Preparing and Testing Hydrogen Gas | Oxygen, What a Flame | Carbon Dioxide, What a Gas | Collecting Gases by Water Displacement | Underwater Fireworks | Flaming Vapor Ramp | The Collapsing Bottle | Solubility of Carbon Dioxide | Solubility of Ammonia |
|---|---|---|---|---|---|---|---|---|---|---|---|
| **Chemicals, continued** | | | | | | | | | | | |
| Thymolphthalein indicator solution, 0.04% | T0079 | | | | | | | | | | 2 mL |
| Universal indicator solution | U0009 | | | 35 mL | | | | | | 2 mL | 2 mL |
| Universal indicator color chart | AP5367 | | | 1 | | | | | | 1 | 1 |
| Zinc, granular | Z0028 | | 15 g | | | | | | | | |
| Zinc, mossy | Z0003 | | | | 6 g | | | | | | |
| **Glassware** | | | | | | | | | | | |
| Beakers | | | | | | | | | | | |
|     100-mL | GP1010 | | | 30 | 30 | | | | | 5 | 6 |
|     150-mL | GP1015 | 15 | | | | | | | | | |
|     1-L | GP1040 | | | | | | | | | 5 | |
| Erlenmeyer flasks | | | | | | | | | | | |
|     250-mL | GP3045 | | | | | | | 1 | | | |
|     1-L | GP3055 | | | | | | | | 1 | | |
| Gas collecting bottle | GP9148 | | | | | 4 | | | | | |
| Gas generation bottle† | AP1558 | | | | | 1 | | | | | |
| Glass plate | AP8264 | | | | | 1 | | | | | |
| Glass tubing, 5 mm O.D. | GP9005 | | | | | 1 | 1 | | | | |
| Graduated cylinders | | | | | | | | | | | |
|     10-mL | GP2005 | 15 | | | | | | | | | |
|     1-L | GP9090 | | | | | | | | 1 | | |
| Stirring rod | GP5075 | 15 | | | 15 | | | | | | |
| Test tubes | | | | | | | | | | | |
|     13 × 100 mm | GP6010 | | 15 | | | | | | | | |
|     15 × 125 mm | GP6015 | 75 | | | | | | | | | |
|     25 × 200 mm | GP6040 | | | 15 | | | | | | | |
| **General Equipment and Miscellaneous** | | | | | | | | | | | |
| Balance, centigram (0.01-g precision) | OB2059 | | | 3 | 3 | | | | | | |
| Bunsen burner | AP5344 | | | 15 | 15 | | | | | | |
| Candles, birthday type | C0226 | | | 1 pkg | 1 pkg | | | | | | |
| Clamp, extension buret | AP8947 | | | | | | | | 1 | | |
| Clamp holder | AP8219 | | | | | | | | 1 | | |

†Includes bottle, two-holed stopper, thistle tube, and bent glass tubing.      *Continued on next page*

# Master Materials Guide

*(for a class of 30 students working in pairs)*                         **Experiments and Demonstrations**

| | Flinn Scientific Catalog No. | Common Gases | Preparing and Testing Hydrogen Gas | Oxygen, What a Flame | Carbon Dioxide, What a Gas | Collecting Gases by Water Displacement | Underwater Fireworks | Flaming Vapor Ramp | The Collapsing Bottle | Solubility of Carbon Dioxide | Solubility of Carbon Dioxide |
|---|---|---|---|---|---|---|---|---|---|---|---|
| **General Equipment and Miscellaneous, continued** | | | | | | | | | | | |
| Clamp, pinchcock-type | AP8211 | | | 15 | | | | | | | |
| Clamp, single buret | AP1034 | | | 15 | 15 | | | 1 | | | |
| Flaming Vapor Ramp Kit | AP6154 | | | | | | | 1 | | | |
| Forceps | AP8328 | 15 | | 15 | | | | | | | |
| Gas collecting classroom equipment kit | AP5951 | | | 1 | 1 | | | | | | |
| Gloves, insulated | SE1031 | | | | | | | | | 1 pair | |
| Litmus paper, neutral | AP7934 | 1 vial | | | | | | | | | |
| Matches, kitchen-type, box | AP2037 | 1 | | 1 | 1 | | | 1 | | | |
| Parafilm, 2″ | AP1500 | 1 | | | | | | | | | |
| Pipet, Beral-type, graduated | AP1721 | | 30 | | 15 | | | | | | |
| Pipet, microtip | AP1719 | | | | | | | | | | 1 |
| Pipet, super jumbo | AP8850 | | | | | | | | | | 5 |
| Pneumatic trough | AP8334 | | | | | 1 | | | | | |
| Razor blade | AB1043 | | 1 | | | | | | | | |
| Rubber stopper, one-holed, size 00 | AP2220 | | 15 | | | | | | | | |
| Rubber stopper, one-holed, size 2 | AP2302 | | | 15 | | | | | | | |
| Rubber stopper, one-holed, size 6 | AP2306 | | | | | | 1 | | | | |
| Rubber stopper, one-holed, size 9 | AP2239 | | | | | | | | 1 | | |
| Rubber tubing, ¼″ I.D. | AP8276 | | | | | 1 | | | | | |
| Silicone grease | AP1095 | | | 1 | 1 | | | | | | |
| Spatula | AP1323 | 15 | | 15 | 15 | | | | | | |
| Straws | AP6025 | | 15 | | | | | | | | |
| Support stand | AP8226 | | | 15 | 15 | | | 1 | 1 | | |
| Test tube rack | AP1319 | 15 | | | | | | | | | |
| Toothpicks, wooden, flat | AP6010 | | 45 | | | | | | | | |
| Tygon tubing, ⅛″ I.D. | AP8373 | | | | | 1 | | | | | |
| Wash bottle | AP1668 | 15 | | | | | | | | | |
| Water, distilled or deionized | W0007<br>W0001 | ✓ | | | | | | | | ✓ | |
| Wooden splints | AP4455 | 45 | | 30 | | | | | | 1 | |

Flinn ChemTopic™ Labs — Chemistry of Gases